WEST VIRGINIA

DAILY
DEVOTIONS
FOR
DIE-HARD
FANS

MOUNTAINEERS

WEST VIRGINIA

MOUNTAINEERS

Daily Devotions for Die-Hard Fans
Available Titles

ACC
Clemson Tigers
Duke Blue Devils
FSU Seminoles
Georgia Tech Yellow Jackets
North Carolina Tar Heels
NC State Wolfpack
Notre Dame Fighting Irish
Virginia Cavaliers
Virginia Tech Hokies

BIG 10
Michigan Wolverines
Michigan State Spartans
Nebraska Cornhuskers
Ohio State Buckeyes
Penn State Nittany Lions

BIG 12
Baylor Bears
Oklahoma Sooners
Oklahoma State Cowboys
TCU Horned Frogs
Texas Longhorns
Texas Tech Red Raiders
West Virginia Mountaineers

SEC
Alabama Crimson Tide
MORE Alabama Crimson Tide
Arkansas Razorbacks
Auburn Tigers
MORE Auburn Tigers
Florida Gators
Georgia Bulldogs
MORE Georgia Bulldogs
Kentucky Wildcats
LSU Tigers
Mississippi State Bulldogs
Missouri Tigers
Ole Miss Rebels
South Carolina Gamecocks
MORE South Carolina Gamecocks
Texas A&M Aggies
Tennessee Volunteers

and *NASCAR*

Daily Devotions for Die-Hard Kids
Available Titles
Alabama, Auburn, Baylor, Georgia, LSU
Miss. State, Ole Miss, Tennessee, Texas, Texas A&M

---

die-hardfans.com

WEST VIRGINIA

DAILY DEVOTIONS FOR DIE-HARD FANS

MOUNTAINEERS

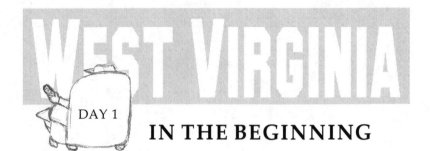

DAY 1

IN THE BEGINNING

Read Genesis 1; 2:1-3.

"God saw all that he had made, and it was very good" (v. 1:31).

Probably no school playing major college football today except West Virginia University can make this claim: William Shakespeare was involved in getting its football program started.

In 1891, two WVU students, Melville Davidson Post and Billy Meyer, convinced some of their buddies to gather at the old baseball grounds in South Morgantown to give this burgeoning sport called football a try. They didn't know anything about the game, but they managed to locate a couple of townfolk who did. One was Robert F. Bivens, who had played at Princeton. He took over as the team's "field captain," the equivalent of the head coach. The second person was Frederick Lincoln Emory, who was appointed by a wary university president to keep an eye on the boys. Emory had played football at Yale.

This is when William Shakespeare showed up. He may well have been a football fan in his day as witnessed by the reference in *Hamlet* to what could have been a bone-crunching tackle: "a hit, a very palpable hit." A production of *Richard III* generated $160 for the football team. The money was used to purchase a football, some spiffy matching uniforms, and a rule book.

The team challenged Washington & Jefferson to a game, an unfortunate choice since the squad from Pennsylvania already

MOUNTAINEERS

had two seasons under its belt. The visitors made the trip up the Monongahela to Morgantown by steamboat. At 3 p.m. on Nov. 28, 1891, football began at WVU. Rain turned to snow about the time the first ball was hiked. Nevertheless, "a sizable number of ladies" were among the large crowd of curious onlookers who stood in the mud to see this new sport for themselves.

Unfortunately, WVU football had an inauspicious beginning. The Mountaineer boys were game and enthusiastic, but they were no match for the more experienced W&J team, which won 72-0.

Beginnings are important, but what we make of them is even more important. Consider, for example, how far the West Virginia football program has come since that regrettable first game.

Every morning, you get a gift from God: a new beginning. God hands to you as an expression of divine love a new day full of promise and the chance to right the wrongs in your life. You can use the day to pay a debt, start a new relationship, replace a burned-out light bulb, tell your family you love them, chase a dream, solve a nagging problem . . . or not.

God simply provides the gift. How you use it is up to you. People often talk wistfully about starting over or making a new beginning. God gives you the chance with the dawning of every new day. You have the chance today to make things right — and that includes your relationship with God.

Every day is a new opportunity. That's the way life is, with a new game every day.
— *Hall of Fame pitcher Bob Feller*

**Every day is not just a dawn; it is
a precious chance to start over or begin anew.**

DAY 2

MIRACLE PLAY

Read Matthew 12:38-42.

"He answered, 'A wicked and adulterous generation asks for a miraculous sign!'" (v. 39)

It was a game no one expected West Virginia's football team to win." When they did, it was dubbed the "Miracle in the Desert."

It wasn't that the Mountaineers didn't belong on the field with the Oklahoma Sooners for the 2008 Fiesta Bowl. Only an upset loss to Pitt kept the team from playing for the national title.

As the players prepared for their BCS match-up against the third-ranked Sooners, though, they received some disconcerting and distracting news. Sixteen days after the regular season ended, head coach Rich Rodriguez walked into the dressing room and informed the team he had taken the job at Michigan and would not be coaching them in the Fiesta Bowl.

Rodriguez left in his wake a team without a head coach that was already "thought to be unstable following the most devastating loss in school history." So uncertain was the situation that it took three days for assistant coach Bill Stewart to be designated the interim head coach for the bowl game. No school "with a true interim head coach had [ever] won a bowl game." As a result, "no one gave West Virginia a chance against the powerful Sooners."

So what happened? The Miracle in the Desert. WVU blew Oklahoma out of the stadium 48-28. The unstoppable Mountaineers rolled up 525 yards of total offense. Freshman running back Noel

Devine stepped in for injured starter Steve Slaton and rushed for 108 yards and two scores. Junior quarterback Pat White threw for 176 yards with two touchdowns and rushed for 150 more.

Fullback Owen Schmitt pulled off the gamebreaker, busting loose for a 57-yard TD run that put WVU up 13-3 in the first half. In the 28-point last half, wide receiver Tito Gonzales caught a 79-yard TD pass, the longest scoring pass in WVU bowl history.

"They never stopped believing," Stewart said of his players and the fans. Even when that belief required a miracle.

Miracles — like pulling off that upset in the desert — defy rational explanation. Escaping with minor abrasions from an accident that totals your car. Or recovering from a so-called terminal illness. Underlying the notion of miracles is the idea that they are rare instances of direct divine intervention that reveal God.

But life shows us quite the contrary, that miracles are anything but rare. Since God made the world and everything in it, everything around you is miraculous. Even you are a miracle. Your life thus can be mundane, dull, and ordinary, or it can be spent in a glorious attitude of childlike wonder and awe. It depends on whether or not you see the world through the eyes of faith. Only through faith can you discern the hand of God in any event; only through faith can you see the miraculous and thus see God.

Jesus knew that miracles don't produce faith, but rather faith produces miracles.

West Virginia pulled off the most improbable victory in school history.
— Writer John Antonik on the 2008 Fiesta Bowl

Miracles are all around us,
but it takes the eyes of faith to see them.

DAY 3

UNEXPECTEDLY

Read Matthew 24:36-51.

*"No one knows about that day or hour, not even the
angels in heaven, nor the Son, but only the Father" (v. 36).*

Their season over, the West Virginia basketball players had scattered for spring break, so the last thing they expected was to win the national title.

After posting a 16-4 record in 1941-42, the team had to hurry back to Morgantown when they received an unexpected invitation to the National Invitational Tournament. At the time, many schools, including West Virginia, preferred the NIT to the less prestigious NCAA Tournament. Interest in the tournament was so widespread that a network of radio stations (the beginnings of the Mountaineer Sports Network) was hastily arranged to carry the games from New York City.

The eighth-seeded Mountaineers took on the top seed, Long Island University, in the opening round. As expected, they had trouble, falling behind 25-18 at halftime. The break didn't improve things as head coach Dyke Raese was locked out of his team's locker room and had to pound on the door to get in to his players.

The Mountaineers caught fire in the last half. A late free throw by center Dick Kesling sent the game into overtime, and WVU went on a 13-4 run to pull off the 58-49 stunner. The upset touched off a wild celebration back in Morgantown. "When they won, it was total bedlam in the streets," said announcer Jack Fleming.

MOUNTAINEERS

Not expecting a long stay, the players and coaches had run out of money. When word of their predicament spread, fans from all over the state began wiring them some funds.

The Mountaineers beat Toledo 51-39 in the second round to set up an unlikely title match against seventh-seeded Western Kentucky. With time running out, Roger Hicks and All-American guard Scotty Hamilton hit free throws to clinch the 47-45 win. Unexpectedly, West Virginia was the national champion.

Life is much like a college game in that just when we think we've got everything figured out and under control, something unexpected happens. About the only thing we can expect from life with any certainty is the unexpected.

God is that way too, suddenly showing up to remind us he's still around. A friend who calls and tells you he's praying for you, a hug from your child or grandchild, a lone lily that blooms in your yard: These are unexpected moments when the divine comes crashing into our lives with such clarity that it takes our breath away and brings tears to our eyes.

But why shouldn't God do the unexpected? The only factor limiting what God can do in our lives is the paucity of our own faith. We should expect the unexpected from God, this same deity who caught everyone by surprise by unexpectedly coming to live among us as a man, and who will return when we least expect it.

We had all gone home for vacation. Our manager had to call around to tell us to come back because we were going to the tournament.
— Forward Walter Rollins on the NIT

**God does the unexpected, like showing up
as Jesus, who will return unexpectedly.**

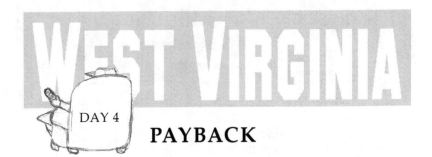

DAY 4

PAYBACK

Read Matthew 5:38-42.

"I tell you, Do not resist an evil person. If someone strikes you on the right cheek, turn to him the other also" (v. 39).

When a reporter asked about payback, head coach Dana Holgorsen's answer included a wink.

In 2013, Maryland drubbed Holgorsen's Mountaineers 37-0. It was the worst beating of his head coaching career. When the two teams met again in 2015, neither Holgorsen nor his players had forgotten. They wanted some payback.

They got it in the first half. With a point to spare, no less.

In an electrifying thirty minutes at Milan Puskar Stadium, WVU exploded out to a 38-0 lead. It was the largest halftime lead the Mountaineers had had since putting 49 on the board in the first half of an 80-7 rout of Rutgers in 2001. On its way to a 45-6 win, WVU set a school record with 37 first downs. The previous record of 36 was set way back in 1923 against Washington & Lee.

Junior quarterback Skyler Howard threw four TD passes, and junior running back Wendell Smallwood rushed for a career-high 147 yards and scored a touchdown in achieving some personal payback. He went into the game with revenge on his mind since the Terrapins had snubbed him and barely recruited him.

"I feel like they felt I wasn't good enough," he said. "So every time I play against them I'm going to make them regret it."

As he met the press following the game, Holgorsen was asked

right away if the 45-6 beatdown constituted payback. He quickly answered, "We rectified that in the first half." Then he winked. In other words, payback was taken care of in the first thirty minutes.

As writer Joey Lomonaco noted, to credit to coincidence that 38-point first-half outburst against the Terps "would be to underestimate Holgorsen." It was indeed payback.

Somebody's done you wrong: that driver who cut you off and sent you to the curb, for example, or a co-worker who took credit with the boss for the work you did. Time to get even? Of course, it is. Hey, what goes around comes around, buddy.

Hold on just a minute, though. There's this little matter of Jesus' insistence that we not seek revenge for wrongs and injuries, no matter how grievous they may be. What we have here is an irreconcilable conflict between how the world says we should act and how God says we are to conduct ourselves.

A close examination of Jesus' unusual command to let it go reveals that it is a blessing, not a call to wimpiness. Consider this: Resentment and anger hurt you and no one else. You're stewing in your own juices, poisoning your own happiness while that other person goes blithely on. The only way someone who has hurt you can keep hurting you is if you're a willing participant.

Jesus ushered in a new way of living when he taught that we are not to seek revenge for wrongs and injuries. What a relief!

Dana Holgorsen expunged the most sullying spot on his resume.
— Writer Joey Lomonaco on payback against Maryland

**Resentment and anger over a wrong injures you,
not the other person, so forget it
— just as Jesus taught.**

DAY 5

A ROARING SUCCESS

Read Galatians 5:16-26.

"So I say, live by the Spirit. . . . The sinful nature desires what is contrary to the Spirit. . . . I warn you, as I did before, that those who live like this will not inherit the kingdom of God" (vv. 16, 17, 21).

Wst Virginia's 1922 football team brought unprecedented success to the program on two fronts: the first-ever undefeated season and the first-ever postseason game.

The squad tossed seven shutouts on its way to a 9-0-1 record. The biggest win was a 9-6 victory over Pitt. (See Devotion No. 69.) The difference was a last-minute dropkick by freshman Armin Mahrt. Mahrt, by the way, turned into a half-year wonder. He was declared ineligible after the seventh game when it was discovered he had played for Dayton the year before.

The successful season earned the Mountaineers a spot in the East-West Bowl in San Diego against Gonzaga. Twenty-seven persons, including nineteen players, made the long trip by train, departing Morgantown on the evening of Dec. 19. They didn't arrive until the 23rd, leaving the Mountaineers with only 48 hours to prepare for the game.

All-American quarterback/halfback Nick Nardacci scored on a 12-yard run in the first quarter. All-American guard Russ Meredith returned an interception 80 yards to make the score 14-0 at halftime. WVU Hall-of-Famer Jack Simons caught a pass from

Nardacci in the third quarter for a 21-0 WVU lead. But then the Mountaineers wilted in the heat and the sandy field they were playing on. Gonzaga rallied but could get no closer than 21-13.

WVU's most successful team had the program's first 10-win season and their first bowl win. The squad didn't arrive home until Jan. 2 after train stops in Los Angeles, San Francisco, Pike's Peak, and Chicago.

Are you a successful person? Your answer, of course, depends upon how you define success. Is the measure of your success based on the number of digits in your bank balance, the square footage of your house, that title on your office door, the size of your boat?

Certainly the world determines success by wealth, fame, prestige, awards, and possessions. Our culture screams that life is all about gratifying your own needs and wants. If it feels good, do it. It's basically the Beach Boys' philosophy of life.

But all success of this type has one glaring shortcoming: You can't take it with you. Eventually, Daddy takes the T-bird away. Like life itself, all these things are fleeting.

A more lasting way to view success is through the lens of the spiritual rather than the physical. The goal becomes not money or backslaps by sycophants but eternal life spent with God. Success of that kind is forever.

If you coach for 25 years and never win a championship but you influence three people for Christ, that is success.
> — *Oklahoma women's basketball coach Sherri Coale*

Success isn't permanent, and failure isn't fatal — unless it's in your relationship with God.

DAY 6

UNBELIEVABLE!

Read Hebrews 3:7-19.

"See to it, brothers, that none of you has a sinful, unbelieving heart that turns away from the living God" (v. 12).

Decades before the WVU-Baylor shootout of 2012 (See Devotion No. 50.), the Mountaineers and Pitt put so many points on the board nobody believed it.

"We came into the game and we thought it would be a cliffhanger and a reasonably low scoring game," declared WVU head coach Gene Corum of the 1965 Backyard Brawl. But the first three times the Mountaineers touched the ball, they scored. "We were leading 21-0 and I thought, 'Oh, we're going to blow them out,'" said wide receiver Bob Dunlevy. "What a mistake that was."

It was a mistake because Pitt kept battling back — and scoring. But so did West Virginia. At halftime, WVU led 28-20. The break did nothing to stop the onslaught. The Mountaineers led 35-34 after three quarters, but then the two teams put an unbelievable 42 points on the board in the final period!

When the offensive fireworks ended only because time ran out, the Mountaineers had a 63-48 win. It was the most points ever scored in a losing effort in major college football history. Corum was led to declare that it was a game you had to see to believe.

Some folks didn't. When a Western Union operator sent out the final score from the press box, the home office suggested he quit drinking during games. They then called Morgantown to personally verify the score. A WVU assistant coach scouting an upcoming opponent said the press at the game was so dismayed by the updates they kept receiving that they sent back, "Please send corrected score."

"I've never seen a game like it in my life," Corum said. It was simply unbelievable.

Much of what taxes the limits of our belief system has little direct effect on our lives. Maybe we don't believe in UFOs, honest politicians, Sasquatch, or the viability of electric cars. A healthy dose of skepticism is a natural defense mechanism that helps protect us in a dog-eat-dog world that all too often has designs on taking advantage of us.

That's not the case, however, when Jesus and God are part of the mix. Quite unbelievably, we often hear people blithely assert they don't believe in God. Or brazenly declare they believe in God but don't believe Jesus was anything but a good man and a great teacher.

All that may sound cool to the smug speaker and his audience. But it's not; it's dangerous. God doesn't fool around with scoffers. He locks them out of the Promised Land, which isn't a country in the Middle East but Heaven itself.

Given that scenario, it's downright unbelievable that anyone would not believe.

It seems unbelievable that a team scoring 48 points could lose.
— Gene Corum on the 1965 Pitt game

Perhaps nothing is as unbelievable as that some people insist on not believing in God or his son.

DAY 7

FIGHT CLUB

Read Hebrews 12:14-17.

"Make every effort to live in peace with all men and to be holy" (v. 14).

There really wasn't anything unusual about the WVU women's defeat of Hawaii to win an early-season tournament in 2013. The postgame trophy presentation was rather interesting, though. As it began, a brawl broke out.

The squad that would win thirty games and the co-championship of the Big 12 took a plane ride to paradise in November for a tournament in Honolulu. They won the first two games and then met host Hawaii in the championship game.

The contest was a thriller. The Mountaineers seemed to be in good shape with a 52-42 lead with 7:35 left, but then the Rainbow Wahine went on a 12-3 run to get close with 39 seconds to play. Brooke Hampton hit a pair of clutch free throws to lock up the 59-56 win. WVU seniors Asya Bussie and Christal Caldwell were named to the All-Tournament Team.

So it was on to the routine trophy presentation ceremony. Only it wasn't so routine this time.

According to a TV report, a Hawaii fan sitting behind the West Virginia bench started heckling the Mountaineer fans who made the trip. The fan then got into a shouting match with members of the WVU staff in the game's final seconds.

As the players lined up on the court for the post-game awards,

MOUNTAINEERS

a West Virginia fan who had had enough grabbed the offending Hawaii fan and the brawl was on. It spilled onto the court.

During the fracas, the wife of Mountaineer coach Mike Carey fainted and Hawaii athletic director Ben Jay was either hit by a chair or punched trying to break it up. Cheryl Carey quickly recovered, but Jay wound up kneeling on the court. He had to be checked on by EMT's and needed about twenty minutes before he was able to walk away under his own power.

Perhaps you've never been in a brawl or a public brouhaha to match that which occurred in Honolulu back in 2013. But maybe you retaliated when you got one elbow too many in a pickup basketball game. Or maybe you and your spouse or your teenager get into it occasionally, shouting and saying cruel things. Or road rage may be a part of your life.

While we do seem to live in a more belligerent, confrontational society than ever before, fighting is still not the solution to a problem. Rather, it only escalates the whole confrontation, leaving wounded pride, intransigence, and simmering hatred in its wake. Actively seeking and making peace is the way to a solution that lasts and heals broken relationships and aching hearts.

Peacemaking is not as easy as fighting, but it is much more courageous and a lot less painful. It is also exactly what Jesus would do.

I saw the fight break out in the corner, so I just leaped over there to try and help break it up. Then I got hit with something in the back.
— Hawaii AD Ben Jay on how he was injured during the melee

Making peace instead of fighting takes courage and strength; it's also what Jesus would do.

DAY 8

FAMILY TIES

Read Mark 3:31-35.

"[Jesus] said, 'Here are my mother and my brothers! Whoever does God's will is my brother and sister and mother'" (vv. 34-35).

During his time as West Virginia's head football coach from 2011-2018, Dana Holgorsen intentionally developed a family-like atmosphere in his football program. In 2016, the approach turned unusually literal; the team included five sets of brothers.

The head man's dad, Steve, was a fixture on the sidelines at practices and games. The coach's son, Logan, spent time at practice shagging balls and tossing them on the sidelines. It was just part of the family atmosphere.

But no college football team in the country matched the literal family atmosphere of the 2016 Mountaineers with their five sets of siblings. They were Jacquez and Jordan Adams (who are twins), Shea and Jonah Campbell, Michael and Brendan Ferns, Chris and Mitch Chugunov, and Ka'Raun and Kyzir White. Actually, the squad featured a sixth set of brothers: assistant coach JaJuan Seider and his baby brother, Ja'HSaun.

Ka'Raun White admitted to benefits from having a brother in the locker room or sharing an apartment. Kyzir and he "talk about everything" in complete honesty, he said.

The downside? Sometimes the coaches confused the brothers, especially the Adams twins and the White brothers. "They've

called me Kyzir a few times now. I'm like, 'that's not my name,'"
Ka'Raun said. "But I don't mind it. My mom does the same thing."

Having five sets of siblings on the team at one time was certainly unusual, but it wasn't necessarily accidental. Coach Ja'Juan Seider had the assignment of acquiring "legacy recruits," players with WVU family ties.

The reasoning behind that approach lay in creating team unity and bonding. As Coach Seider put it, "Who can you trust more than your brother?" Or even a band of brothers?

Some wit said families are like fudge, mostly sweet with a few nuts. You can probably call the names of your sweetest relatives, whom you cherish, and of the nutty ones too, whom you mostly try to avoid at a family reunion.

Like it or not, you have a family, and that's God's doing. God cherishes the family so much that he chose to live in one as a son, a brother, and a cousin.

One of Jesus' more radical actions was to redefine the family. No longer is it a single household of blood relatives or even a clan or a tribe. Jesus' family is the result not of an accident of birth but rather a conscious choice. All those who do God's will are members of Jesus' family.

What a startling and downright wonderful thought! You have family members out there you don't even know who stand ready to love you just because you're part of God's family.

It's pretty cool that we have a bunch of brothers here.
— Wide receiver Ka'Raun White on WVU's band of brothers.

**For followers of Jesus, family comes not from
a shared ancestry but from a shared faith.**

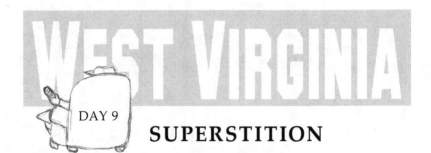

DAY 9

SUPERSTITION

Read 1 Samuel 28:3-20.

"Saul then said to his attendants, 'Find me a woman who is a medium, so I may go and inquire of her'" (v. 7).

From licking his right thumb to making his wife stay home from the game, WVU head coach Art "Pappy" Lewis was a walking bundle of superstitions when it came to the Pitt game.

Sports Illustrated chronicled Lewis' rituals before the 1955 Backyard Brawl. The writer noted that the coach always wore the same brown suit before the game, the one he had worn when WVU upset the Panthers in 1952. When the writer asked Lewis about the health of his team, he said it was just fine. Then he rushed over to one of Pitt Stadium's wooden goalposts and tapped on it for good luck.

Lewis and assistant coach Ed Shockey would usually take in a movie the week of the game to relax a little and try to ease their anxiety. As the flick headed for the finish, they would slip out, never seeing the end.

On Friday mornings before the game, Lewis always strolled down High Street chatting with local store owners. He was on his way to the Hotel Morgan for a cup of coffee. At any time during his morning constitutional, Lewis "might stop, lick his right thumb and stamp it three times into the palm of his left hand. He would also sometimes make an imaginary X in the air and compulsively spit through it."

Lewis' wife, Mary Belle, had to remain in Morgantown for the Pitt game. She always had to wear the same dress and listen to the same transistor radio that had "blared out" WVU's 1953 defeat of Penn State.

At the team hotel after the last pre-game practice, Lewis sought out the same friend he had talked to before the 17-7 win over Pitt in '53. Later, he took his 12-year-old son, Johnny, out for a lobster dinner. Of course, the pair had dined on lobster before the Mountaineer wins over Pitt in 1952 and '53.

Black cats are right pretty. A medium is a steak. A key chain with a rabbit's foot wasn't too lucky for the rabbit. Unlike Art Lewis, about as superstitious as you get is to extend a blessing by declaring "God bless you" when someone sneezes.

You look indulgently upon good-luck charms, horoscopes, tarot cards, astrology, palm readers, and the like; they're really just amusing and harmless. So what's the problem? Nothing as long as you conduct yourself with the belief that superstitious objects and rituals can't bring about good or bad luck. You aren't willing to let such notions and nonsense rule your life.

The danger of superstition lies in its ability to lure you into trusting it, thus allowing it some degree of influence over your life. In that case, it subverts God's rightful place.

Whether or not it's superstition, something does rule your life. It should be God — and God alone.

I had one superstition: to touch all the bases when I hit a home run.
— *Babe Ruth*

**Superstitions may not rule your life, but
something does; it should be God and God alone.**

TIME FOR A CHANGE

Read Romans 6:1-14.

"Just as Christ was raised from the dead through the glory of the Father, we too may live a new life" (v. 4).

Before he ever said a word, Don Nehlen let his players know things had changed around Morgantown.

Nehlen, of course, is a college football legend. With a 149-93-4 record, he is the winningest coach in Mountaineer football history. He was the National Coach of the Year twice and was inducted into the College Football Hall of Fame in 2005. From 1980-2000, he led WVU to fifteen winning seasons and thirteen bowl games.

The program that through the 2018 season had the twentieth-most wins in major college football history was not in very good shape when Nehlen took over in 1980. The Mountaineers had suffered through four straight losing seasons.

When Nehlen told Bo Schembechler, his boss at Michigan, he was going to take the West Virginia job, Schembechler told him he was crazy. "I just think this is a big mistake," he said. Nehlen responded by pulling out a map. "Bo, there are a ton of football players within 300 miles of Morgantown," he asserted. "I got a feeling I can get me 15 of those guys a year."

Armed with that conviction, Nehlen headed east.

Quarterback Oliver Luck, who in 2010 was named the school's athletic director, was at the first meeting the new coach had with his team. Nehlen walked in and encountered guys "slouched

MOUNTAINEERS

down in their chairs" with "baseball caps pulled down over their heads" and their "feet propped up on empty table tops." As Luck described the scene, "It had the look of a room full of losers."

Nehlen took one look, walked over to one of those players with his feet on a table, and kicked them both to the floor. He immediately served notice that more than the name on the coach's office had changed around town. In Nehlen's second season, WVU won nine games, was ranked in the top 20, and whipped Florida 26-6 in the Peach Bowl.

Like some football programs, anyone who asserts no change is needed in his or her life just isn't paying attention. Every life has doubt, worry, fear, failure, frustration, unfulfilled dreams, and unsuccessful relationships in some combination. The memory and consequences of our past often haunt and trouble us.

Simply recognizing the need for change in our lives, though, doesn't mean the changes that will bring about hope, joy, peace, and fulfillment will occur. We need some power greater than ourselves or we wouldn't be where we are.

So where can we turn to? Where lies the hope for a changed life? It lies in an encounter with the Lord of all Hope: Jesus Christ. For a life turned over to Jesus, change is inevitable. With Jesus in charge, the old self with its painful and destructive ways of thinking, feeling, loving, and living is transformed.

A changed life is always only a talk with Jesus away.

Right then we realized it was going to be a different regime.
— Oliver Luck when Don Nehlen kicked a player's feet off a table

**In Jesus lie the hope and the power
that change lives.**

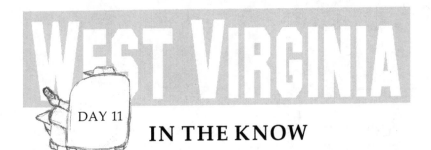

DAY 11

IN THE KNOW

Read John 4:27-42.

"They said to the woman, . . . 'Now we have heard for ourselves, and we know that this man really is the Savior of the world'" (v. 42).

His team was ranked number one in the nation, but UNLV's head coach knew before the game even started that his boys were in big, big trouble.

With his 439-276 record achieved through 24 seasons in Morgantown (1978-2002), Gale Catlett is the winningest coach in West Virginia basketball history. His 1981-82 team reeled off a 23-game win streak on the way to a 27-4 record, a ranking of 14th in the country, and a berth in the NCAA Tournament.

Four starters returned, including the team's three top scorers. Thus, basketball fever ran high in Morgantown, especially after Catlett upgraded the schedule and brought several powerhouses to the Coliseum. One of those was UNLV. The Runnin' Rebels were ranked number one in the country when they arrived for a nationally televised game on CBS on Feb. 27, 1983.

Quite simply, the place went nuts. Students camped outside the Coliseum for more than two days to get a seat "for the biggest game they had ever seen in their lives." When senior guard Greg Jones, an All-American and a two-time Atlantic 10 Conference Player of the year, walked into the arena at 10 a.m., more than three hours before tipoff, the student section was full.

MOUNTAINEERS

UNLV head coach Jerry Tarkanian knew something was up. He realized he "was taking his team into an ambush" when the Rebels arrived at the Holiday Inn next to the Coliseum. From his bus window, he could see the long line of students camped out in 30-degree weather. All night long, he could hear the excited students as he unsuccessfully tried to sleep.

Sure enough, behind Jones' 32 points, WVU built a nine-point halftime lead, led by as many as fifteen points in the second half, and won 87-78. The overjoyed students stormed the court.

Tarkanian had pretty much known it was coming.

He just knew in the same way you know certain things in your life. That your spouse loves you, for instance. That you are good at your job. That tea should be iced and sweetened. That a bad day fishing or hunting is still better than a good day at work. You know these things even though no mathematician or philosopher can prove any of this on paper.

It's the same way with faith in Jesus: You just know that he is God's son and the savior of the world. You know it in the same way that you know the Mountaineers are the only team in the world worth pulling for.

But it isn't just that you know Jesus with every fiber of your being, with all your heart, your mind, and your soul. There's more. Because you know Jesus, you are his and he knows you. And that is all you really need to know.

How did you ever talk me into coming here to play, Gale?
— Jerry Tarkanian to Gale Catlett before the WVU-UNLV game

**A life of faith is lived in certainty and conviction:
You just know you know.**

DAY 12

THE BIG TIME

Read Revelation 21:22-27; 22:1-6.

"They will see his face, and his name will be on their foreheads. . . . And they will reign for ever and ever" (vv. 22:4, 5c).

St. Ambrose. Iowa Wesleyan. Valdosta State. Mississippi College. Wingate. They were all stops on Dana Holgorsen's long and winding journey to the big time.

Holgorsen grew up in Mount Pleasant, Iowa. "It was hard to get in trouble around there," he said. "Everybody knew everybody." No football was offered until he was in the seventh grade.

Holgorsen played his college ball at St. Ambrose University and at Iowa Wesleyan, both small NAIA colleges in Iowa. One of the assistant coaches at Iowa Wesleyan was Mike Leach. The head coach was Hal Mumme, later the boss of the Kentucky program.

After he graduated, Holgorsen followed Mumme to Valdosta State before taking a job at Mississippi College. For several seasons, he "toiled in obscurity" at Mississippi College and Wingate University. The worst part about the Mississippi College job for Holgorsen was that the coaches had to plant shrubs and flowers around the campus during the summers.

When Leach got the head job at Texas Tech, he called Holgorsen. The conversation was brief: "Come here," Leach said. Holgorsen was on his way to the big time with stints as the offensive coordinator at Tech, Houston, and Oklahoma State. At OSU, he lived in a hotel and nightly studied videos of football plays "into the early morning while drinking some of the nearly a dozen sugar-free Red Bulls he consume[d] daily."

West Virginia athletic director Oliver Luck visited Holgorsen during the 2010 season with a proposal. He would come to West Virginia as the offensive coordinator and the coach-in-waiting for when Bill Stewart left. He accepted.

On June 10, 2011, Holgorsen took the final step into the big time when he became WVU's head football coach. He compiled a 61-41 record before taking the Houston job after the 2018 season.

We often look around at our current situation and dream of hitting the big time. We might look longingly at that vice-president's office or daydream about the day when we're the boss, maybe even of our own business. We may scheme about ways to make a lot of money, or at least more than we're making now. We may even consciously seek out fame and power.

Making it big is just part of the American dream. It's the heart of that which drives immigrants to leave everything they know and come to this country.

But all of this so-called "big-time" stuff we so earnestly cherish is actually only small potatoes. If we want to speak of what is the real big-time, we better think about God and his dwelling place in Heaven. There we not only see God and Jesus face to face, but we reign. God puts us in charge. Now that's the big time.

It was bad football, a bunch of slow little white kids running around.
— Dana Holgorsen on the football he played growing up.

**Living with God, hanging out with Jesus,
and reigning in Heaven — now that's big time.**

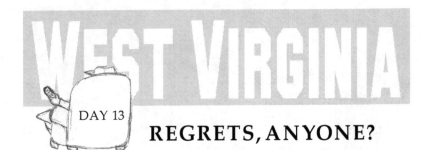

REGRETS, ANYONE?

Read 2 Corinthians 7:8-13.

"Godly sorrow brings repentance that leads to salvation and leaves no regret" (v. 10).

By any yardstick, Major Harris had a brilliant college football career at WVU. His regrets about it came in the way it ended.

Harris quarterbacked the Mountaineers from 1987-89. In 1988, he directed the team to its first-ever undefeated, untied regular season and a berth in the Fiesta Bowl for the national championship. He was an All-American in 1989 and finished third in the voting for the Heisman Trophy. He was the first quarterback in major college football history to pass for more than 5,000 yards and rush for more than 2,000 yards. In 2009, he was inducted into the College Football Hall of Fame.

ESPN's Ivan Maisel credited Harris with being the player who turned West Virginia into a national program.

After his junior season, Harris decided to turn pro. At a press conference in February of 1990, he confirmed a rumor that he would sign with a Los Angeles sports agent.

"I had no money," he said. He saw other players whose resumes weren't nearly as flashy as his making the leap to the pros. "You are basically following suit," he said.

Harris came to regret the way everything went down. "You've got people in your ear telling you different things," he said. "I wasn't getting the right advice from the right people, but you don't realize that when you're young."

Harris was drafted in the twelfth round by the Los Angeles Raiders, but he never played in the NFL, lasted only one year in the Canadian Football League, and ended his pro career playing Arena Football.

"Looking back on it," he said, "I probably wouldn't have come out. . . . The way I did it was wrong. . . . The one thing I regret most is that I didn't really go to Coach [Don] Nehlen and sit down and listen to what he thought about [my turning pro]."

In their classic hit "The Class of '57," the Statler Brothers served up some pure country truth when they sang, "Things get complicated when you get past 18." That complication includes regrets; you have them; so does everyone else: situations and relationships that upon reflection we wish we had handled differently.

Feeling troubled or remorseful over something you've done or left undone is not necessarily a bad thing. That's because God uses regrets to spur us to repentance, which is the decision to change our ways. Repentance is essential to salvation through Jesus Christ. You regret your un-Christlike actions, repent by promising God to mend your ways, and then seek and receive forgiveness for them.

The cold, hard truth is that you will have more regrets in your life. You can know absolutely, however, that you will never ever regret making Jesus the reason for that life.

Leaving school early was a mistake [Major] Harris still regrets.
— *John Antonik in* The Backyard Brawl *(2012)*

**Regrets are part of living, but you'll
never regret living for Jesus.**

DAY 14

THE FALL

Read Genesis 3:1-7, 21-24.

*"When the woman saw that the fruit of the tree was good
. . ., she took some and ate it. She also gave some to her
husband" (v.6).*

The most decorated offensive lineman in WVU history pulled
off one of his best plays as he stumbled and tried not to fall.

From 2003-06, Dan Mozes was a four-year starter for the Mountaineers. Named first-team All-Big East three times, he spent his
first two seasons at left guard before moving to center. His senior
season he was a consensus All-American and won the Rimington
Trophy, presented annually to college football's top center.

The coaches decided to move Mozes to center the week of the
Maryland game of 2005. It didn't start out too well as his first two
snaps were "less than stellar." They were like rockets. Head coach
Rich Rodriguez called for line coach Rick Trickett to move Mozes
back to guard. "Give him one more series to let him cool down,"
Trickett said. Mozes said he was never sure that he cooled down
but quarterbacks Pat White and Adam Bednarik were such good
athletes "they were able to keep those snaps on their chests."

West Virginia lost once in 2005 and landed in the Sugar Bowl
against SEC champion Georgia. The Mountaineers led 31-28 and
faced a third-and-10 inside their own 10 late in the game. On the
play Rodriquez called, Mozes' job was to block the middle linebacker. As the play developed, though, he stumbled and the line-

backer rushed past him. About to fall, Mozes managed to lunge backward and brush the linebacker enough to spring White for a first down. West Virginia went on to drive for the game-winning touchdown and a 38-35 win that remains one of the program's watershed victories. John Antonik of WVU's athletic department wrote that Mozes' block as he tried to avoid falling "probably ended up winning it for the Mountaineers."

Falling is an overarching metaphor for Christianity in that the faith views the world as fallen. That is, neither we nor the planet itself are what they were when God created them. Disobedience to God effected the change and brought both sin and evil into the world. They've never left, in large part because we continue to repeat Adam and Eve's original misstep.

That is, as the first twosome did, we desire to be like God (v. 5). Even more arrogantly, we want to be God. So we claim autonomy, supplant God's rules with our own, seek out the forbidden, and generally deny God's will for our lives. We live in a state of perpetual disobedience, which, just as with Adam and Eve, results in separation from God.

This is sin, the use of our God-given freedom to assert independence from our creator. This is The Fall; we have lost the Garden. Through God's awesome grace, though, we have a way back to the Garden and to righteousness. Jesus Christ is that way.

The greatest accomplishment is not in never falling, but in rising again after you fall.

— *Vince Lombardi*

**The Fall brought sin and death to the creation;
Jesus brings righteousness and life to it.**

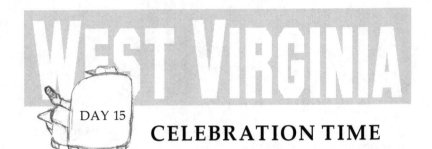

CELEBRATION TIME

Read Luke 15:1-10.

"There is rejoicing in the presence of the angels of God over one sinner who repents" (v. 10).

Bill McKenzie's kick on the last play of the game touched off a raucous celebration — except for defensive tackle Chuck Smith, who found a unique and extremely tame way to celebrate.

On Nov. 8, 1975, Bobby Bowden's underdog team battled Pitt to a 14-14 deadlock into the fourth quarter. A tie appeared to be a sure thing after the WVU defense forced a punt to midfield with 10 seconds on the clock. Quarterback Dan Kendra knew the team needed some sort of miracle to get within range of a McKenzie field goal, so he told tight end Randy Swinson to turn his pattern upfield. "Let's give it a shot, what the heck?" Kendra said.

With Pitt defenders in his face, Kendra lofted a pass down the sideline in Swinson's general direction. He found the ball and made the catch, getting knocked out of bounds at the Pitt 22 with four seconds on the clock. That brought on McKenzie, a walk-on sophomore who hadn't tried a field goal until two weeks before, which made WVU the last school in major-college football to attempt a field goal. His kick was perfect, right down the middle.

By the time McKenzie's boot landed in the stands, some WVU students were already celebrating on the field. A large mass of humanity quickly converged on the players. "I thought I was going to die," Swinson said as his teammates piled on him.

MOUNTAINEERS

Smith ran onto the field to join in the celebration but noticed a student walking dazedly around. He said he was looking for his glasses. Smith found a busted pair on the ground and handed them to the student. "Thanks, man! This is the greatest day of my life," he said. Teammates later kidded Smith that at one of the most exciting moments in WVU football history, he gave a student his glasses.

WVU just won. You got that new job or that promotion. You just held your newborn child in your arms. Life has those grand moments that call for celebration. You may jump up and down and scream in a wild frenzy at Milan Puskar Stadium or share a quiet, sedate candlelight dinner at home — but you celebrate.

Consider then a celebration that is beyond our imagining, one that fills every niche and corner of the very home of God and the angels. Imagine a celebration in Heaven, which also has its grand moments.

Those grand moments are touched off when someone comes to faith in Jesus. Heaven itself rings with the joyous sounds of the singing and dancing of the celebrating angels. Even God rejoices when just one person — you or someone you have introduced to Christ? — turns to him.

When you said "yes" to Christ, you made the angels dance.

I got a copy of the highlight video, and it shows the pile going on and you can see me giving the kid his glasses.
— *Chuck Smith on celebrating the win over Pitt*

**God himself joins the angels in heavenly
celebration when even a single person
turns to him through faith in Jesus.**

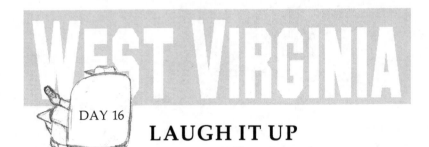

DAY 16

LAUGH IT UP

Read Genesis 21:1-7.

"Sarah said, 'God has brought me laughter, and everyone who hears about this will laugh with me'" (v. 6).

Irrepressible and a born showman, Hot Rod Hundley left fans dazzled and delighted with his skills and laughing at his antics.

Hundley played for WVU from 1954-57. A two-time, first-team All-American, he was the fourth player in NCAA history to score more than 2,000 points. The Mountaineers made it to the NCAA Tournament each of his three varsity seasons, their first times in the big dance. His jersey number 33 was retired in 2010, and in 2016, a bronze statue of him was unveiled at the WVU Coliseum.

A tough competitor who liked to win, Hundley nevertheless believed every game should be showtime. He dribbled the ball behind his back and between his legs, bounced it off his knees, rolled it down his arm, and often took hook shots at the free throw line. Since it wasn't illegal at the time, he would hang on the rim waiting for a lob pass from a teammate.

Against William & Mary in 1955, Hundley missed a layup and trotted over to the W&M bench and sat down. "Get off the bench!" the opposing coach screamed. "I'm tired," Hundley replied. When the coach yelled at the ref to get Hundley off his bench, Hot Rod told him to find a rule that said he couldn't sit there. When WVU got the rebound, he said, "OK, I'm gone." A teammate passed him the ball and he scored on a layup.

MOUNTAINEERS

He sometimes led the home crowd in cheering "We want Hundley!" when he had been taken out of a game. He often acknowledged applause during a game, and the more he received the bolder his antics became.

"He was a piece of work. He was a nut," declared All-Southern Conference forward Jim Sottile of his teammate who loved to leave 'em laughing.

Stand-up comedians are successful because they find humor in the world, and it's often hard for us to do that. "Laughter is foolish," an acerbic Solomon wrote in Ecclesiastes 2:2, his angst overwhelming him because he couldn't find much if anything in his world to laugh at.

We know how he felt. When we take a good look around at this world we live in, can we really find much to laugh at? It seems everywhere we look we find not just godlessness but ongoing and pervasive tragedy and misery.

Well, we can recognize as Sarah did that in God's innumerable gifts lie irresistible laughter. The great gift of Jesus provides us with more than enough reason to laugh no matter our situation. Through God's grace in Jesus Christ, we can laugh at death, at Satan, at the very gates of hell, at the world's pain.

Because they are of this world, our tears will pass. Because it is of God, our laughter will remain — forever.

To [Hot Rod] Hundley, basketball was an opportunity to put on a show, and that seemed to tickle fans across the state.
— Writer Roland Lazenby

Of the world, sorrow is temporary;
of God, laughter is forever.

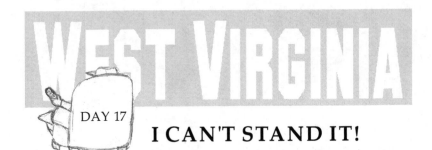

DAY 17

I CAN'T STAND IT!

Read Exodus 32:1-20.

"[Moses'] anger burned and he threw the tablets out of his hands, breaking them to pieces at the foot of the mountain" (v. 19).

The 2016 Mountaineer football team showed against Brigham Young that it might get frustrated but it sure wouldn't quit.

In Landover, Md., on Sept. 24, WVU held on to beat the Cougars from out west 35-32 in a game WVU running back Rushel Shell called "the tensest game I've ever been in." With 11:27 left, quarterback Skylar Howard connected with senior wide receiver Daikiel Shorts, Jr., for a 9-yard touchdown pass. The score propelled WVU into what seemed like a comfortable 35-19 lead.

Head coach Dana Holgorsen was having none of it. After the game, he admitted that he "kind of threw a fit" about then. In no uncertain terms, he told his players to stay ready because he knew the game wasn't over. He was dead right about that.

If the players needed any reminder about what could happen, they had only to look back at the closing seconds of the first half. It apparently ended with WVU up 21-10, but the refs got together and ruled the Cougars had spiked the ball with one second left. BYU kicked a field goal to make it a one-score game at 21-13.

That odd ending to the half left Holgorsen concerned about more twists and turns in the game's last 11:27. What did happen was enough frustration to last the Mountaineers a whole season.

MOUNTAINEERS

While West Virginia's offense sputtered in frustration, the Cougars scored twice to make it 35-32. WVU finally answered with a drive to the BYU 4 with 2:36 left. The game was over, right? But a miscommunication between Howard and his center resulted in a fumble. As frustrated WVU fans and players watched in disbelief, the Cougars quickly moved in position to tie the game or win it.

They didn't do either one. Cornerback Maurice Fleming finally ended the day's frustration with an interception at the WVU 2.

The traffic light catches you when you're running late for work or your doctor's appointment. The bureaucrat gives you red tape when you want assistance. Your daughter refuses to take her homework seriously. Makes your blood boil, doesn't it?

Frustration is part of God's testing ground that is life even if much of what frustrates us today results from manmade organizations, bureaucracies, and machines. What's important is not that you encounter frustration — that's a given — but how you handle it. Do you respond with curses, screams, and anger? Or do you take a deep breath, lift a silent prayer, and settle into calm persistence and patience?

It may be difficult to imagine Jesus stuck in traffic or waiting for hours in a long line in a government office. It is not difficult, however, to imagine how he would act in such situations, and, thus, to know exactly how you should respond. No matter how frustrated you are.

A lot of things happened that put that victory in jeopardy.
— Dana Holgorsen on the frustrating final minutes of the BYU win

**Frustration is a vexing part of life,
but God expects us to handle it gracefully.**

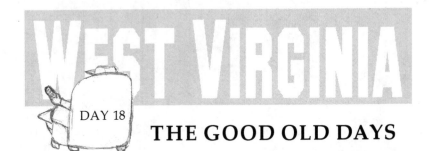

THE GOOD OLD DAYS

Read Psalm 102.

"My days vanish like smoke; . . . but you remain the same, and your years will never end" (vv. 3, 27).

By 1975, the good old days for Mountaineer Field "were in the rearview mirror."

That's the year WVU athletic director Leland Byrd received the alarming report that the facility was falling down. It wasn't news to those who used it regularly. Christened with a 21-6 win over West Virginia Wesleyan in 1924, the stadium was closed in 1979 and demolished in 1987. It really wasn't a moment too soon.

The Astroturf "was terrible and hard," according to linebacker Mike Dawson, and thus was a hazard to the players. The bleachers were rotting, the white paint on the concrete was chipped and faded, and large chunks of concrete lay on the ground.

Not only in disrepair, the facility was also outdated. So little room existed on the sidelines that the players could have conversations with fans during a game. "You could sit there and talk to somebody about your math class," recalled All-American linebacker Darryl Talley (1979-82). "As a quarterback, you couldn't warm up on the sidelines," said Oliver Luck (1979-81), who set school records for career touchdowns and completions. There was no room. Fans in the first three rows often shouted at the players to take a knee so they could see the game.

There was dirt on the floor of what passed for the weight room at the time. The space was so small that position players had to lift in small groups. "Could you imagine being in a cave?" Talley asked. "It was like a dungeon." "It was like you were in an alley in New York City at night time," recalled 1983 captain Dave Oblak.

The team meeting room was so small that head coach Frank Cignetti found it easier to assemble his team in the visitors' locker room to talk to them. Players would get taped in the training room and then walk across the field for the meeting.

The good old days at old Mountaineer Field were long gone before it was.

It's a brutal truth that time just never stands still. The current of your life sweeps you along until you realize one day you've lived long enough to have a past. Like the memories of wins at old Mountaineer Field, part of your past you cling to fondly. The stunts you pulled with your high-school buddies. Your first apartment. That dance with your first love. Those "good old days."

You hold on relentlessly to the memory of those old, familiar ways because of the stability they provide in our uncertain world. They will always be there even as times change and you age.

Another constant exists in your life too. God has been a part of every event in your life that created a memory because he was there. He's always there with you; the question is whether you ignore him or make him a part of your day.

A "good old day" is any day shared with God.

We used to call it the snake pit.
    — Linebacker Darryl Talley on old Mountaineer Field

**Today is one of the "good old days"
if you share it with God.**

DAY 19

HOMELESS

Read Matthew 8:18-22.

"Jesus replied, 'Foxes have holes and birds of the air have nests, but the Son of Man has no place to lay his head'" (v. 20).

For a brief period in 2011, West Virginia's athletic program was in effect homeless, casting about for a place in which to play.

On Sept. 18, Pitt and Syracuse submitted their applications to join the ACC. Coupled with earlier defections by Boston College, Miami, and Virginia Tech, Big East football had pretty much been gutted. The existence of the league itself was in doubt.

But where could West Virginia go? The athletic department had long ago conceded the ACC would not extend an invitation. The SEC was more interested in Missouri. As writer Mike Casazza put it, "The only league that wanted WVU was the Big East, but WVU wanted out in a bad way."

But then the Big 12, itself ravaged by conference realignment, extended an invitation to WVU. The geography was awful, but "the excitement about a new life in a new league trumped everything else." A press conference was set for Oct. 26 to make the big announcement. Overnight, though, the deal was off. "The Mountaineers were wanted and ecstatic and optimistic one day and then stranded and rejected and depressed the next."

It seems a U.S. senator who had graduated from Louisville and wanted his alma mater in the Big 12 had tossed enough threats around to give the conference pause. On Friday, though, the league came back around and again invited and accepted WVU.

So the Mountaineers were home free? Not yet. League honchos suddenly realized WVU would be the eleventh member, which would make scheduling extremely difficult. Forty-eight more uncertain hours passed before it was finally all over. (Missouri jumped to the SEC, leaving ten members in the misnamed league.)

Effective July 1, 2012, WVU had a home in the Big 12.

WVU's teams weren't truly homeless, of course, but homelessness is all too real in America. The bag lady pushing a shopping cart; the scruffy guy with a beard and a backpack holding a cardboard sign. If you look closer at them, you may see a desperate woman with children fleeing violence, or veterans haunted by their combat experiences, or sick or injured workers.

Few of us are indifferent to the homeless when we're around them. They often raise quite strong passions, whether we regard them as a ministry or an odorous nuisance. They trouble us, perhaps because we realize that we're only one catastrophic illness and a few paychecks away from joining them. They remind us how tenuous our hold is upon the material success we so value.

But they also stir our compassion because we serve a Lord who — like them — had no home, and for whom, the homeless, too, are his children.

The Mountaineers were merely going through the motions [of negotiating with the Big East] as they tried to find a new home.
— Writer Mike Casazza

Because they, too, are God's children,
the homeless merit our compassion, not our scorn.

DAY 20

DREAM WORLD

Read Joshua 3.

"All Israel passed by until the whole nation had completed the crossing on dry ground" (v. 17b).

Growing up, Ginny Thrasher had dreams of being an Olympic champion. She just had the wrong sport.

Thrasher wanted to be a figure skater. She competed through high school, dancing and twirling to music. "I kind of dreamed of going to the Olympics in it," she said. But one day, she begged her grandfather to take her hunting though she had never fired a rifle before. She liked it and learned to shoot from her father, who's retired from the Air Force. When Thrasher bagged her first white-tailed deer, shooting become a passion.

She joined her high school's air rifle team and then enrolled at West Virginia in the fall of 2015. In leading the Mountaineers to the 2016 national title, their fourth straight, she became the first freshman in NCAA history to sweep the individual titles.

Thrasher made the 15-member U.S. shooting team for the 2016 Olympics in Rio de Janeiro as its youngest shooter at 19. She was ranked 23rd in the world and thus was a long shot to medal. One writer said, she "wasn't considered a serious medal threat by most, not with so many experienced shooters in the field."

All the young Mountaineer did was go out on Aug. 6 and make her lifelong Olympic dream come true. She opened the finals of the 10-meter air rifle competition with a bulls-eye, and the seven other shooters never stood a chance. Thrasher won the gold, the first medal awarded in Rio, in the process beating two Chinese shooters who had won six Olympic medals between them. Her score set an Olympic record.

She didn't have much time to celebrate her dream's coming true. She competed in the 50-meter rifle event and flew home to begin her sophomore year at WVU, landing about twenty hours before her fall semester began with an 8:30 a.m. physics class.

No matter how tightly or doggedly we may cling to our dreams, devotion to them won't make them a reality. Moreover, the cold truth is that all too often dreams don't come true even when we put forth a mighty effort. The realization of dreams generally results from a head-on collision of persistence and timing.

But what if our dreams don't come true because they're not the same dreams God has for us? That is, they're not good enough and, in many cases, they're not big enough.

God calls us to great achievements because God's dreams for us are greater than our dreams for ourselves. Could the Israelites, wallowing in the misery of slavery, even dream of a land of their own? Could they imagine actually going to such a place?

The fulfillment of such great dreams occurs only when our dreams and God's will for our lives are the same. Our dreams should be worthy of our best — and worthy of God's involvement in making them come true.

This is beyond my wildest dreams.
— Olympic gold medalist Ginny Thrasher on her win in Rio

If our dreams are to come true, they must be worthy of God's involvement in them.

GREAT EXPECTATIONS

Read John 1:43-51.

"'Nazareth! Can anything good come from there?'
Nathanael asked" (v. 46).

West Virginia supporters generally didn't have high expectations when Art "Pappy" Lewis was hired as the head football coach. What they got was the program's second golden era.

Lewis first sought the Mountaineer job in 1948 when Bill Kern resigned after five seasons and 24 wins. Athletic director Roy "Legs" Hawley went with Dudley DeGroot instead. DeGroot left after two seasons, taking the head job at New Mexico State.

At the time, the average life expectancy of a West Virginia football coach was a mere two and a half years. With a career head coaching record of only 11-17, Lewis didn't seem like the man to change those expectations. But he was familiar with the program from his time at Washington & Lee when he lost to the Mountaineers three straight times. He believed there was talent in those West Virginia mountains and he could bring it to Morgantown.

Lewis let his interest in the job be known but heard nothing from WVU representatives for a couple of weeks. Then he received a sudden call asking for a meeting. He was offered the job.

Lewis didn't find much talent on campus, and his 1950 team won only twice. But he was recruiting well. The 1951 team relied heavily on freshman but still managed a 5-5 record. WVU's second "Golden Era" of football began in 1952. Over the next six

MOUNTAINEERS

seasons, WVU went 44-13-1 and won five Southern Conference titles. The wins included a streak of 30 straight conference games.

Lewis' legend "took on mythical proportions when *Life* magazine came to Morgantown to spend a week with him." He was so popular at one point a football board game was named after him.

Art "Pappy" Lewis exceeded all expectations.

The blind date your friend promised looked like Ryan Reynolds or Jennifer Lawrence but instead resembled Cousin Itt or an extra in a zombie flick. Your vacation of a lifetime that went downhill after the lost luggage. Often your expectations are raised only to be dashed. Sometimes it's best not to get your hopes up; then at least you have the possibility of being surprised.

Perhaps most devastating of all to your self-esteem, however, is when you realize that you are the one not meeting the expectations other people have for you. The truth is, though, that you aren't here to live up to what others think of you. Jesus didn't; in part, that's why they killed him. But he did meet God's expectations for his life, which was all that really mattered.

Because God's kingdom is so great, God does have great expectations for any who would enter, and you should not take them lightly. What the world expects from you is of no importance; what God expects from you is paramount.

I always will feel that they wanted me to take it for a year or two while they looked around for someone else. But I fooled them.
— *Art 'Pappy' Lewis on being hired as WVU's football coach*

You have little if anything to gain from meeting the world's expectations of you; you have all of eternity to gain from meeting God's.

TRUE CHAMPIONS

Read 1 Corinthians 9:24-27.

"Everyone who competes in the games goes into strict training. . . . [W]e do it to get a crown that will last forever" (v. 25).

The Big East championship and a BCS bowl were slipping away until a Mountaineer with only one good hand made a play.

Everything the team had hoped for back in August was still on the table when 8-3 WVU hosted South Florida in the final game of the 2011 regular season. But the Mountaineers had to win.

It went well — for a while. Receiver Tavon Austin returned a kickoff 90 yards to give West Virginia a 20-10 lead. But then came a horrific stretch of three turnovers in eleven plays that the Bulls turned into points. With 9:49 to go, South Florida led 27-20.

"I'm not going to lie to you. That was ridiculous," asserted defensive end Julian Miller, who played in a school-record 52 games. "That hurt. It really did."

But quarterback Geno Smith and the offense responded with a game-tying drive with just over five minutes to play. South Florida promptly returned the kickoff to the WVU 41. Linebacker Najee Goode called it a "punch in the face." When the Bulls converted on third-and-4, it was pretty much over. A rather routine field goal would win it unless somebody made a play.

A Mountaineer basically playing with one hand did just that. Goode caused a fumble, but then watched in dismay as a teammate ran past the ball and the Bulls' offensive linemen closed in. Then linebacker Doug Rigg showed up, a starter who had missed two games when he broke his hand against LSU and had surgery. He played the rest of the season with a protective cast and had trouble catching a pass. He could, however, corral the ball.

Tyler Bitancurt kicked a game-winning field goal as time ran out. When UConn lost, the Mountaineers were Big East champs.

That South Florida game is an apt metaphor for the life we lead as Christians. When it seemed their hopes had been dashed and their faith in themselves had been misplaced, the Mountaineers stayed focused, rededicated themselves to their purpose, worked harder, and kept the faith.

Such is the life of a Christian. It is a wonderful life — the only really worthwhile one — but it isn't an easy life. Paul spoke of beating his body and making it a slave; that's certainly not very appealing. No, the well-lived Christian life requires a keen sense of purpose, discipline, hard work, and preparation. Which sounds a lot like a championship football team.

Very few of us get the chance to compete for an NCAA national title. All of us, however, who put our faith in Jesus Christ compete for a championship. Rather than a trophy, we receive a crown. Rather than sycophantic adulation, we earn God's pleasure and a nod of approval from Jesus Christ.

We are true champions — for all of eternity.

The guy on the team with one good hand got the ball?
— Najee Goode on Doug Rigg's unlikely fumble recovery

**Those who follow Christ all the way to Heaven
are life's true champions.**

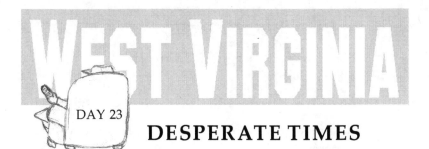

DAY 23

DESPERATE TIMES

Read Mark 5:22-43.

"Seeing Jesus, [Jairus] fell at his feet and pleaded with him, 'My little girl is dying. Please come'" (vv.22-23).

Wendell Smallwood didn't play football for love of the game. He played it out of desperation.

"Football definitely saved my life," he once said. That's because football gave the young Smallwood a way not only to avoid his surroundings but to eventually escape them. Football, he said, gave him the determination to succeed.

He grew up in "the rough neighborhoods of Wilmington," Del. But he had friends who like him were determined to get out and a coach willing to make it possible. He was Dwayne Thomas, who made sure his kids were so focused on football and academic success "they were too tired to hang out at parties even if they wanted to."

Thomas treated football like a college program, keeping the players at school for twelve hours every day. His kids would often bunk together, sleeping on the floor at their various homes to support and encourage each other and to share their dreams.

It wasn't easy. When he was 13, Smallwood was among some kids at a convenience store when trouble broke out. Though he was simply in the wrong place and not a perpetrator, Smallwood was sentenced to community service and ordered to write his mother a letter of apology. Smallwood never forgot his misery at seeing his mother in court. He promised her he would be OK.

Football helped him make good on that promise. A high school star, Smallwood signed with West Virginia and arrived in the fall of 2013. As a junior in 2015, he rushed for 1,519 yards, the fourth-highest total in school history. The desperate times behind him, he was taken by the Philadelphia Eagles in the 2016 NFL draft.

As with Jairus and the bleeding woman, the Bible is replete with stories echoing the old aphorism "There are no atheists in foxholes." That is, nothing drives people to God like desperation.

But that's true not just in the desperate straits of combat. We all experience desperate times in our lives. All too often it is only when we reach that point of no return and little hope that we turn to God in prayer. Consider, for instance, the public officials who either disdain or outlaw public prayer but then who are among the first to call for prayer in times of national or local tragedy.

Christians who pray daily no matter their circumstances can perhaps justly react with cynicism to the prayers of those who ignore God except when they don't have anything else. But we would do well to remember that, as C.S. Lewis once observed, God is "unscrupulous." His point is that God uses any means at his disposal to bring his wayward children back into his arms.

If desperation drives some to their knees, there is always the hope that what they find there will bring them back again.

Many kids on [my] teams played out of desperation, [not] for recreation.
— High school coach Dwayne Thomas

Desperate times can be blessings if they
force us to turn to and depend upon God.

DAY 24

COMEBACK KID

Read Luke 23:26-43.

"Then he said, 'Jesus remember me when you come into your kingdom.' Jesus answered him, 'I tell you the truth, today you will be with me in paradise'" (vv. 42-43).

Bob Huggins' college coaching career was over and done with, kaput, history. Funny thing about that.

On Aug. 23, 2005, the president of the University of Cincinnati gave Huggins an ultimatum: Either resign as the men's basketball coach or be fired. He resigned. What was in essence a nasty firing that had nothing to do with victories left Huggins, as Yahoo's Dan Wetzel put it, "slightly radioactive. . . . Many schools were never going to touch him." Wetzel wrote, "Almost no one comes back from a college firing." At the time, only Eddie Sutton could truly be said to have resuscitated his career at a major school.

So how did Huggins' handle what was supposedly a dark time in his life? "It wasn't as bad a low point as you all try to make it out to be," he said. "It's kind of fine."

As Wetzel wrote, Huggins didn't just deal with being fired; "he kind of reveled in it. He was a millionaire who got to spend a year enjoying life." But he wasn't coaching and with Sutton the only precedent, the odds were long that he would ever do so again in the big time.

Nevertheless, Huggins' confidence never wavered. "I knew I would coach again," he said.

After only one season away from the game, he got a chance for a comeback when Kansas State hired him in 2006. The Wildcats won 23 games. And then Huggins' alma mater called.

In 2007, he came home to West Virginia. Through the 2017-18 season, his teams had averaged 23 wins a campaign. The 2009-10 team set a school record with 31 wins. When the squad made the Final Four, Huggins had matched Sutton's rare achievement.

He had made his comeback as a big-time college coach.

As Bob Huggins can tell you, life will have its setbacks whether they result from personal failures or from forces and people beyond your control. Being a Christian and a faithful follower of Jesus Christ doesn't insulate you from getting into deep trouble.

Maybe financial problems suffocated you. A serious illness put you on the sidelines. Or perhaps your family was hit with a great tragedy. Life is a series of victories and defeats. Winning isn't about avoiding defeat; it's about getting back up to compete again. It's about making a comeback of your own.

When you avail yourself of God's grace and God's power, your comeback is always greater than your setback. You are never too far behind, and it's never too late in life's game for Jesus to lead you to victory, to turn trouble into triumph. As it was with the penitent criminal crucified with Jesus, it's not how you start that counts; it's how you finish.

The guy has fallen down more times than he can count. Each time he's gotten back up and kept coaching
— Writer Dan Wetzel on Bob Huggins' comebacks

**No matter the circumstances in your life,
you can begin a comeback by turning to Jesus.**

DAY 25

REVELATION

Read Isaiah 53.

"But he was pierced for our transgressions, he was crushed for our iniquities; the punishment that brought us peace was upon him, and by his wounds we are healed" (v. 5).

Early on, Don Nehlen showed that as a football coach he had a little bit of the prophet in him.

Sept. 6, 1980, was one of the most exciting days in WVU's long football history. A new season began, which was exciting enough. But it began with a new head coach and a brand new stadium packed with 50,000 people. Before the game, Nehlen, that new coach, sat on a platform with West Virginia Governor Jay Rockefeller and John Denver.

The day finished on an exciting note as the Mountaineers beat Cincinnati 41-27. The wins didn't come easily that season, though. The team lost three games by five or fewer points and limped into the Rutgers game on Nov. 15 with a 5-5 record.

Looking for some kind of an edge against a pretty good band of Scarlet Knights, Nehlen asked Jack Fleming, the West Virginia radio announcer, to make a tape of what the game's opening series would sound like. The coach told Fleming that the Mountaineers would kick off and hold Rutgers on two running plays. Then on third down, the defense would grab an interception. So Fleming cut the tape just as the head coach had asked. When the players heard it, they went stark raving nuts.

They were still fired up when they kicked off. Sure enough, Rutgers ran the ball the first two downs for short gains. Then on third down, their quarterback dropped back to pass. "I think that about 11 Mountaineers leapt in the air to intercept the football," Nehlen said. And they did — just as the tape had predicted.

The team rode the momentum of that start to a 24-15 upset.

In our jaded age, we have pretty much relegated prophecy to dark rooms in which mysterious women peer into crystal balls or clasp our sweaty palms while uttering some vague generalities. At best, we understand a prophet as someone who predicts future events as Don Nehlen seemed to do with his Rutgers tape.

Within the pages of the Bible, though, we encounter something radically different. A prophet is a messenger from God, one who relays divine revelation to others.

Prophets seem somewhat foreign to us because in one very real sense the age of prophecy is over. In the name of Jesus, we have access to God through our prayers and through scripture. In searching for God's will for our lives, we seek divine revelation. We may speak only for ourselves and not for the greater body of Christ, but we do not need a prophet to discern what God would have us do. We need faith in the one whose birth, life, and death fulfilled more than 300 Bible prophecies.

I could not believe how real the tape sounded. It made the hairs on my arms stand up. The players thought so, too.
— Don Nehlen on Jack Fleming's Rutgers tape

Persons of faith continuously seek
a word from God for their lives.

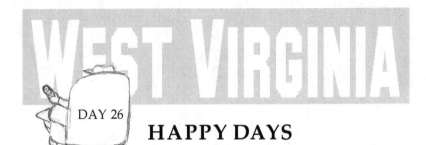

DAY 26

HAPPY DAYS

Read Nehemiah 8:1-3, 9-12.

"Do not grieve, for the joy of the Lord is your strength"
(v. 10b).

Carl Kinder was asked to do something no other West Virginia football player has ever done, and he wasn't too happy about it.

Kinder was the kicker and punter for head coach Gene Corum's 1963 team back in the days when the Mountaineers still played in the Southern Conference. He was also a three-year letter winner as a catcher for coach Steve Harrick's baseball team.

After kicking in 1963, Kinder broke an ankle while making a tackle in the '64 opener against Richmond (a 20-10 win). He was medically redshirted. Healed up by season's end, he considered kicking in the Liberty Bowl, "but I was completely unpracticed and it would have cost me one season of eligibility," he said.

He returned to kick in 1965 and '66. For his career he booted fourteen field goals and sixty of sixty-one PAT's. As a senior, he was able to play for Jim Carlen in his first season and was coached by offensive coordinator Bobby Bowden.

In 1963, Kinder asked the coaches for a specific jersey number. He wanted a number from among zero, one, three, or seven. "I am a Christian and Bible teachings preferred one of those," he explained. He didn't get it. Instead, he got a number so weird it had never been worn before and never would be again: 100.

"I was disappointed and surprised," Kinder admitted. Then he learned why such a strange jersey number would even exist: It was in observance of the Mountain State's 100ᵗʰ birthday in 1963. After that, Kinder didn't complain though he still would have been happier with one of the numbers that witnessed to his faith.

In 1966, the staff ditched the jersey "because they thought I was getting too much publicity wearing No. 100," Kinder said. Did he get the number he wanted? Nope. He got 10.

A widespread theology preaches that happiness and prosperity are signs of faithfulness. It's certainly seductive, this notion that with faith comes happiness.

But it reduces God to a servant or a vending machine existing only to meet our wishes, coughing up whatever it takes to make us happy. This theology also means that if I am not happy, then God has failed.

Yes, God wants us to be happy. God gave us our life to enjoy; God created this world for us to enjoy; he sure doesn't need it. In God's economy, though, we are to be happy but only with conditions. If it is sin that makes us happy, God doesn't want it for our lives. Moreover, if it is some thing in our lives, some circumstance in our lives, or even some person in our lives that makes us happy, then God is indifferent about it.

God is so good to us that he wants more for us than happiness, which is temporal and worldly. For us, he wants joy, which is eternal and divine. Joy is found only in God through Jesus Christ.

I just didn't realize it was the state's birthday.
— Carl Kinder on why he was initially unhappy with the number 100

**Happiness simply isn't good enough for us
because it doesn't depend upon Jesus Christ.**

DAY 27

YOUNG BLOOD

Read Jeremiah 1:4-10.

"The Lord said to me, 'Do not say, 'I am only a child' . . .
for I am with you and will rescue you" (vv. 7a, 8).

David Sills V shattered the taboo that decreed college football scholarships could not be offered to middle-school athletes. He was 13 and in the seventh grade when he received his first offer.

At WVU in 2017, Sills, a wide receiver, led the nation with 18 touchdown catches. He was a first-team All-America. As a senior in 2018, he hauled in another 15 TD passes to lead the Big 12. He was a second-team All-America and ended second in the WVU record book with 35 career touchdown catches.

But it wasn't as a receiver that Sills earned a reputation as a football phenom but as a quarterback. When quarterback guru Steve Clarkson watched Sills in a special workout, he said he had never seen anything like it. "This was not normal," he said. "I started to rethink, 'How young is too young?'" Sills was 10.

Then-USC head coach Lane Kiffin watched a YouTube clip of Sills and said, "I thought I was looking at a 10th or 11th grader." Sills was only 13, but after talking with Clarkson, Kiffin made the unprecedented scholarship offer that garnered national attention.

It didn't work out. An injury Sills' junior season forced him to change his passing technique, and he missed most of his senior season with a broken ankle. New USC boss Steve Sarkisian made it clear Sills no longer fit in the Trojans' plans. "Once the model of a perfect quarterback, Sills had become damaged goods."

But WVU head coach Dana Holgorson still saw promise, and Sills came to Morgantown. Holgorson moved him to receiver in 2015, and the freshman saw some action. In the spring of 2016, though, Sills left for a community college to give quarterback one more try. He was good but no offers came in, and Holgorson invited him to come back. Sills did, and the former quarterback phenom — all grown up now — became a Mountaineer legend.

While our media do seem obsessed with youth, most aspects of our society value experience and some hard-won battle scars. Life usually requires us to spend time on the bench as a reserve, waiting for our chance to play with the big boys and girls. Unlike David Sills V, you probably rode some pine in high school. You entered college as a freshman. You started out in your career at an entry-level position.

Paying your dues is traditional, but that should never stop you from doing something bold and daring right away. Nowhere is this more true than in your faith life.

You may assert that you are too young and too inexperienced to really do anything worthwhile for God. Those are just excuses, however, and God won't pay a lick of attention to them when he issues a call.

After all, the younger you are, the more time you have to serve.

We thought about [Sills' age]. At the same time, we had never seen anybody look like that.
— *Lane Kiffin on offering then-13-year-old David Sills a scholarship*

Youth is no excuse for not serving God;
it just gives you more time.

DAY 28

STRANGE BUT TRUE

Read Philippians 2:1-11.

"And being found in appearance as a man, he humbled himself and became obedient to death — even death on a cross!" (v. 7)

From a dead fish on the court to a head coach for a week, the WVU men's basketball program has seen some strange times.

"One of the most famous shots in the history of WVU basketball" was partially blocked. With only seven seconds left in the second round of the 1998 NCAA Tournament, Cincinnati hit a jump shot to take a 74-72 lead. Point guard Jarrod West hustled downcourt and with one second left jacked up a 30-footer for the 75-74 win. Two things were strange about the shot: It was a bank shot, and a Bearcat got a hand on it After the game, a Cincinnati player verified that a teammate got "a piece of it."

In 1970, the Mountaineers beat Pitt 67-66 in overtime when forward Larry Woods put back an offensive rebound with twelve seconds left. The great Wil Robinson scored 17 points. The home-standing Pitt fans were so disgruntled by his play that one lobbed a dead fish onto the court as Robinson was shooting a free throw.

The final game of the 1993 regular season (an 82-67 win at St. Bonaventure) was interrupted by a bomb scare. The building was evacuated in the middle of a snowstorm. With nowhere else to go, the two teams hopped aboard the WVU team bus, one team on each side. They amicably waited for the bomb-sniffing dogs to check out the arena.

In April 2002, WVU basketball had a head coach for a week. On Feb. 13, Gale Catlett resigned after 24 seasons as the boss Mountaineer. Bowling Green's Dan Dakich was announced as the new head coach and stayed in Morgantown a week. Then, strangely enough, after a week of turning his team's workouts into boot camp, he up and returned to Ohio and his old job.

Some things in life are so strange their existence can't really be explained. How else can we account for the sport of curling, tofu, that people go to bars hoping to meet the "right" person, the proliferation of tattoos, and the behavior of teenagers? Isn't it strange that someone would hear the life-changing message of salvation in Jesus Christ and then walk away from it?

And how strange is that plan of salvation that God has for us? Just consider what God did. He could have come roaring down, annihilating everyone whose sinfulness offended him, which, of course, is pretty much all of us. Then he could have brushed off his hands, nodded the divine head, and left a scorched planet in his wake. All in a day's work.

Instead, God came up with a totally novel plan: He would save the world by becoming a human being, letting himself be humiliated, tortured, and killed, thus establishing a kingdom of justice and righteousness that will last forever.

It's a strange way to save the world — but it's true.

It sounds strange: Many champions are made champions by setbacks.
— Olympic champion Bob Richards

It's strange but true: God allowed himself
to be killed on a cross to save the world.

DAY 29

JUST PERFECT

Read Matthew 5:43-48.

"Be perfect, therefore, as your heavenly Father is perfect"
(v. 48).

The Mountaineer Field scoreboard said it all: "PERFECT."

On Nov. 19, 1988, the West Virginia Mountaineers were poised to make gridiron history. They were 10-0 and hosted Syracuse in the last game of the season. With a win, they would complete the first undefeated, untied season in the program's history and lock down their first-ever berth in the BCS championship game.

The Mountaineers grasped history from the get-go, driving 69 yards for a touchdown on their first possession. After an interception by linebacker Theron Ellis, WVU covered 22 yards in two plays for a 14-3 lead. Syracuse never recovered. The perfect season went in the history books with a resounding 31-9 win.

Senior cornerback Dave Lockwood noted that after the game, the players first "went around and saluted everybody and headed back to the locker room." There the coaches tried to share the moment with their 11-0 team, but the players couldn't hear them. They were drowned out by the racket from the more than 65,000 fans who were still in their seats a half hour after the game ended. They were demanding a curtain call. They got it.

With the scoreboard flashing "PERFECT," the players returned to the field. "The stadium [was] still packed," Lockwood said.

MOUNTAINEERS

"Wow! To come out of the locker room and see that is probably my biggest memory of the year."

"Not a fan had left," said secondary coach Steve Dunlap. "And it was cold. It was late in the year. We went all around the field to shake the hands of the fans, and it was sensational. I had seen some things before but never anything like that."

All in all, it was just perfect.

Nobody's perfect; we all make mistakes every day. We botch our personal relationships; at work we seek competence and not perfection. To insist upon personal or professional perfection in our lives is to establish an impossibly high standard that will eventually destroy us physically, emotionally, and mentally.

Yet that is exactly the standard God sets for us. Our love is to be perfect, never ceasing, never failing, never qualified — just the way God loves us. And Jesus didn't limit his command to goody-two-shoes types and preachers. All of his disciples are to be perfect as they navigate their way through the world's ambiguous definition and understanding of love.

But that's impossible! Well, not necessarily, if to love perfectly is to serve God wholeheartedly and to follow Jesus with single-minded devotion. Anyhow, in his perfect love for us, God makes allowance for our imperfect love and the consequences of it in the perfection of Jesus.

If we chase perfection, we can catch excellence.
— *Vince Lombardi*

**In his perfect love for us, God provides a way
for us to escape the consequences
of our imperfect love for him: Jesus.**

DAY 30

A SURE THING

Read Romans 8:28-30.

"We know that in all things God works for the good of those who love him, who have been called according to his purpose" (v. 28).

One WVU sports information associate was so sure of a Pitt win that he left the press box for his post-game interviews before the game ended. He missed "one of the most bizarre finishes in Backyard Brawl history."

John Antonik joined the staff of West Virginia's sports information department in 1991 as an associate. He assumed the post of Director of Digital Media in 1999. During his tenure, he and the department have won awards for excellence, and he has written several books on WVU athletics.

In 1994, Antonik was fretting as the Backyard Brawl headed toward what was a sure and bitterly disappointing finish for the Mountaineers. WVU had apparently squandered a 25-point first-half lead when Pitt took a 41-40 lead with 54 seconds left.

"What player or coach is going to want to come out and talk to reporters after this debacle?" Antonik wondered as he dutifully headed toward the bowels of Pitt Stadium for his interviews with what were now certain to be the losers.

In a bathroom, he splashed water on his face and adjusted his tie when he heard a commotion in the hallway. He discovered that a uniformed policeman had just kicked a garbage can as he uttered a few choice expletives about Pitt's defensive backs.

"Excuse me, officer, what just happened?" Antonik asked. "The kid from West Virginia scored a touchdown," he growled.

A dismayed Antonik rushed outside to find it was true. With 23 seconds left, wide receiver Zach Abraham had hauled in a 60-yard touchdown strike from quarterback Chad Johnston. The game was over, and the 47-41 West Virginia win was a sure thing.

Football games aren't played on paper. That is, the outcome isn't a sure thing. You attend a West Virginia game expecting — or at least hoping — that the Mountaineers will win, but you don't know for sure. If you did, why bother to go? Any football game worth watching carries with it an element of uncertainty.

Life doesn't get played on paper either, which means that living, too, comes bearing uncertainty. You never know what's going to happen tomorrow or even an hour from now. Oh, sure, you think you know. Right now you may be certain that you'll be at work Monday morning, that you'll have a job next month, and that you'll be happily and comfortably married to the same spouse five years from now. Life's uncertainties, though, can intervene at any time and disrupt those sure things you count on.

Ironically, while you can't know for sure about this afternoon, you can know for certain about forever. Eternity is a sure thing because it's in God's hands. Your unwavering faith and God's sure promises lock in a certain future for you.

My difficult job had now become impossible.
— Sure of a WVU loss, John Antonik on his '94 post-game interviews

Life is unpredictable and tomorrow is uncertain;
only eternity with or without God is a sure thing.

DAY 31

CALLING IT QUITS

Read Numbers 13:25-14:4.

"The men who had gone up with him said, 'We can't attack those people; they are stronger than we are'" (v. 13:31).

Pat White was so ready to quit football that his dad brought a glove to a game so he could begin a baseball career right away.

WVU played Louisville on Oct. 15, 2005, (See Devotion No. 77.) and a discouraged White was on the bench. As All-American kicker Pat McAfee put it, "Everyone knew that once Pat White got his chance on the field, he was going to be special."

But White's chances on the field were in fact diminishing. He had competed with sophomore Adam Bednarik for the starting job, and the two had pretty much split playing time in the season's first five games. But in a win over Rutgers the previous week, White had barely seen the field, finishing the game with one pass and two rushes.

After that game, White called his dad, and they talked over how discouraged and frustrated he was. The youngster got what turned out to be life-changing advice. His dad told him to go out and practice hard for the Louisville game. Give it everything he had. If at the end of the week he felt the same way, White senior would bring his son's baseball glove to the game, and he could head off for a pro baseball career.

What happened, of course, is Mountaineer lore. Bednarik was

injured in the game, and White led an astounding comeback. He was the starter through the 2008 season and rewrote the school record book. He set an all-time NCAA record for career rushing yards (since broken) and was the first starting quarterback in NCAA history to win four bowl games. He led the Mountaineers to an era of unprecedented success with a 28-4 record.

It's difficult not to wonder: Would White have really quit had Bednarik not been injured that Saturday against Louisville?

Did you ever quit a high-school sports team because you knew you weren't going to get to play? Bail out of a relationship that was obviously going nowhere? Walk away from a job that didn't offer much of a future? Quitting may be painful, but sometimes it's the most sensible way to minimize your losses. At times, you may well give up on something or someone.

In your relationship with God, however, you should remember the people of Israel, who quit when the Promised Land was theirs for the taking. They forgot one fact of life you never should: God never gives up on you.

That means you should never, ever give up on God. No matter how tired or discouraged you get, no matter that it seems your prayers aren't getting through to God, no matter what — quitting on God is not an option.

He is preparing a blessing for you, and in his time, he will bring it to fruition — if you don't quit on him.

I was almost ready to give up and give in.
— Pat White the week of the 2005 Louisville game

Whatever else you give up on in your life, don't give up on God; he will never ever give up on you.

DAY 32

DAZED AND CONFUSED

Read Genesis 11:1-11.

"There the Lord confused the language of the whole world" (v. 9a).

The Mountaineers once played a game that ended in such confusion that no one was certain what the final score was.

Though West Virginia was the favorite against Pitt in 1947, the team headed into the game in total disarray. Head coach Bill Kern surprisingly handed in his resignation the Tuesday morning before the game on Saturday. Equally surprising, university president Irvin Stewart quickly accepted it.

Empty seats and frigid temperatures greeted the teams, but the West Virginia players rose above it all to dominate Pitt. Not without some confusion, though.

In the second quarter, Richard Hoffman booted a rare field goal for a 10-zip WVU lead. Guard Gene Corum, who coached the Mountaineers from 1960-'65, blocked a punt to set up the kick. He thought he had fallen on the ball for a touchdown until the players untangled and the snow was swept away. He was sitting on the 5-yard line and not in the end zone.

West Virginia led 17-0 when the Panthers blocked a punt as the final seconds ticked off. The ball scooted on the snow toward the goal line and encountered a throng of Mountaineer rooters who had already converged on the goal post to claim it as their own. Somebody in the crowd hauled off and kicked the ball.

MOUNTAINEERS

First-year broadcaster Jack Fleming was up in the press box trying to figure out what was happening in the crowd and the fog down below. He had problems of his own as a disappointed Pitt partisan punched Fleming's spotter, who responded by throwing a chair at the fan. The press box crew dispatched an emissary to both dressing rooms and discovered that a safety had been awarded during all that confusion. The final score was 17-2.

Though it sometimes doesn't seem that way, confusion is not the natural order of things. God's universe — from the brilliant arrangement of DNA to the complex harmony of a millipede's legs to the dazzling array of the stars — is ordered. God's act of creation was at its most basic the bringing of order out of chaos.

So why then is confusion so pervasive in our society today? Why do so many of us struggle to make sense of our lives, foundering in our confusion over everything from our morals and values to our sexual orientation and our sense of what is right and what is wrong? The lesson of the Tower of Babel is instructive. That which God does not ordain he does not sustain. Thus, confusion is not the problem itself but is rather a symptom of the absence of God's will and God's power in our lives.

At its most basic, confusion for the children of God is a sense of purposelessness. It fills the void that is created by a lack of intimacy with God.

The goal posts were going down, there were people on the field, and the game ended 17-0.
— Jack Fleming on the confusion at the end of the '47 Pitt game

**Keeping confusion at bay
requires keeping God near.**

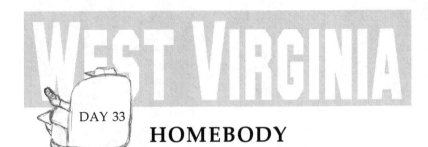

DAY 33

HOMEBODY

Read 2 Corinthians 5:1-10.

"We . . . would prefer to be away from the body and at home with the Lord" (v. 8).

A 1956 Ford convertible and a good friend helped keep a homesick Jerry West from leaving WVU before his career ever started.

"The most famous athlete to ever wear the Gold and Blue," Jerry West is a West Virginia and basketball icon. From 1957-60, he was the leading scorer on three of West Virginia's greatest basketball teams. The 1957-58 team went 26-1; the 1958-59 squad came within a basket of winning the national title. He was a three-time All-America whose jersey number 44 was retired in 2005. In 2007, the school unveiled a statue of him outside the WVU Coliseum.

In the fall of 1956, though, West struggled to adjust to college life. He had grown up in Chelyan, West Virginia, with its population of about five hundred. It was an insulated upbringing. "We never ever went anyplace out of town," said West's sister, Patricia West Noel. "We didn't have a car. We didn't have the money."

West arrived in Morgantown in the summer to allow for some adjustment time. But when the full body of six thousand students hit the campus, he was "met with a horrific sense of isolation." He was overwhelmed; in other words, the small-town boy was homesick. "Every day was a struggle to get through," he later said.

He soon decided to hop a southbound train and return home. So he started walking the tracks that ran near campus, waiting

MOUNTAINEERS

for a train to come by. But fellow freshman and roommate Willie Akers intervened. The two had become friends at Boys State the previous summer. Akers called head coach Fred Schaus, who went to the tracks and convinced West to return to campus.

West's salvation that first year was Akers' car. The two of them rolled around in style in a 1956 Ford convertible. West "settled in a bit [and] found a little comfort." He may still have suffered from bouts of homesickness, but he didn't try to leave WVU again.

Home is not necessarily a matter of geography. It may indeed be that place you share with your family, whether it's in West Virginia or Los Angeles. Or you may feel at home when you return to Morgantown, wondering why you were so eager to leave in the first place. Maybe the home you grew up in still feels like an old shoe, a little worn but comfortable and inviting.

It is no mere happenstance that among the circumstances of life that we most abhor is that of being rootless. That dread results from the sense of home God planted in us. Our God is a God of place, and our place is with him.

Thus, we may live a few blocks away from our parents and grandparents or we may relocate every few years, but we will still sometimes feel as though we don't really belong no matter where we are. We don't; our true home is with God in the place Jesus has gone ahead to prepare for us. We are homebodies and we are perpetually homesick.

I was terribly disillusioned by being away from home.
— Jerry West as a college freshman

We are continually homesick for our real home,
which is with God in Heaven.

ULTIMATE MAKEOVER

Read 2 Corinthians 5:11-21.

"If anyone is in Christ, he is a new creation; the old has gone, the new has come!" (v. 17)

Reed Williams wasn't always the intimidating warrior he was at West Virginia. He had to make himself into one — twice.

From 2005-09, Williams was a standout linebacker for the Mountaineers. He was three times named to the All-Big East squad. He was the Defensive Player of the Game in the 48-28 clobbering of Oklahoma in the 2008 Fiesta Bowl, still considered by many to be "the greatest bowl victory — and arguably the greatest victory — in WVU football history."

The image of Williams perhaps known to and loved by WVU fans is best illustrated by the Rutgers game in 2007. On the field, he was the ultimate warrior. He led the defense with thirteen tackles in the 31-3 win.

On the sideline, he also presented the image of the ultimate warrior. There he stood with his flaming red hair matted by the driving rain, which also pushed streaks of eye black down both his cheeks. He was "quite a sight to behold." "The eye black's all part of it," he said. "I feel like a warrior when I put it on."

But Reed Williams didn't always feel like or look like a football warrior. He was, as he put it, "a little fat boy. You guys watch 'King of the Hill?' I looked like Bobby Hill." But he was always athletic, so the "little fat boy" went to work and made himself over into a lean, tenacious football star.

Williams had to make himself over once again at West Virginia. After that Fiesta Bowl and three seasons of college football, his shoulders were a mess. He reluctantly had surgery and then tried to come back in 2008. The pain and his limited range of movement were too much. He reluctantly agreed to sit out the season.

Williams hated every minute of being on the sideline, but he didn't waste the time. Through rehab, he made himself over, this time reshaping himself from a wounded warrior into a healthy one. He was back on the field in 2009 for his senior season.

Ever considered a makeover? TV shows show us how changes in clothes, hair, and makeup and some weight loss can radically alter the way a person looks. But these changes are only skin deep. Even with a makeover, the real you — the person inside — remains unchanged. How can you make over that part of you?

By giving your heart and soul to Jesus — just as you give up your hair to the makeover stylist. You won't look any different; you won't dance any better; you won't suddenly start talking smarter. The change is on the inside where you are brand new because the model for all you think and feel is now Jesus. He is the one you care about pleasing.

Made over by Jesus, you realize that gaining his good opinion — not the world's — is all that really matters. And he isn't the least interested in how you look but how you act.

Don't think that the way you are today is the way you'll always be.
— Legendary Georgia football coach Vince Dooley

Jesus is the ultimate makeover artist; he can make you over without changing the way you look.

WEST VIRGINIA

FATHERS AND SONS

Read Matthew 3:13-17.

"A voice from heaven said, 'This is my Son, whom I love; with him I am well pleased'" (v. 17).

Bonde Zereoue sent his son, Amos, out of the house and away from home. He did it to save him.

From 1996-98, Amos Zereoue established himself as one of the most outstanding running backs in WVU football history. He set a school record in career rushing yards (since broken). He was the first player in school history to rush for more than 1,000 yards in three straight seasons. Three times he was first-team All-Big East. On his first play from scrimmage at WVU, he went 69 yards for a touchdown. He went on to play for the Steelers from 1999-2003. In 2015, he was inducted into the WVU Sports Hall of Fame.

Amos was born in Ivory Coast and came to the U.S. with his father, Bonde, and younger sister when he was 7. His dad was a commercial photographer who settled in Hempstead, Long Island.

By the time Amos was in junior in high school, though, he was running with a bad crowd. He cut classes, stayed out late, and frequently got into fights. The senior Zereoue decided it was time to take some drastic action to rescue his son from the destructive path he was headed down.

He sent his son to Hope for Youth, a home for troubled boys. "I had to do something to save him," the father explained. "He hated me for it, but I told him, 'I'm doing it for your own good.'"

MOUNTAINEERS

In a different environment, Amos quickly straightened out. He found his way to the football field and to a changed life. He also soon came to understand why his father had done what he did. When he turned 16, he decided to stay at the boys' home rather than return to Hempstead. "I wanted to see it through," he said.

Our contemporary society largely belittles and marginalizes fathers and their influence upon their sons. Fathers are all too often perceived as either ridiculous or extraneous, necessary only to effect pregnancy. After that, they can leave and everybody's better off.

But we need look in only two places to appreciate the enormity of that misconception. One is our jails, packed with males who lacked the influence of fathers in their lives as they grew up. The other is the Bible. God — being God — could have chosen any relationship he desired between Jesus and himself, including society's approach of irrelevancy. Instead, the most important relationship in all of history was that of father-son.

God obviously believes a close, loving relationship between fathers and sons, such as that of Bonde and Amos Zereoue, is crucial. For men and women to espouse otherwise or for men to walk blithely and carelessly out of their children's lives constitutes disobedience to the divine will.

Simply put, God loves fathers. After all, he is one.

I knew my father was right.
  — Amos Zereoue on his dad's decision to send him to a boys' home

**Fatherhood is a tough job, but a model
for the father-child relationship is found
in that of Jesus the Son with God the Father.**

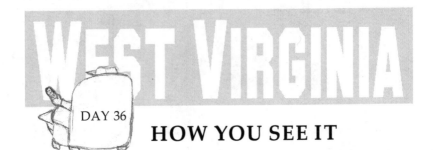

DAY 36

HOW YOU SEE IT

Read John 20:11-18.

"Mary stood outside the tomb crying" (v. 11).

After some trying times, Will Grier discovered a new perspective at West Virginia that let him enjoy both football and life again.

Grier was WVU's starting quarterback in 2017 and 2018. He threw for 7,354 yards, third all-time in the Mountaineer record book. His 71 career touchdown passes are second only to Geno Smith. In 2018, he finished fourth in the Heisman balloting.

Grier burst onto college football in 2015 at Florida when he paired up with receiver Antonio Callaway for a 67-yard touchdown play that beat Tennessee 28-27 with only 1:39 on the clock. Seven days later, his time as a Gator was over.

He tested positive for a performance-enhancing drug called Ligandrol, which he took to treat muscle wasting. "I should have consulted with the trainer about what I was doing," Grier said. "I was careless. I was ignorant." He was also made aware that he didn't fit into new head coach Jim McElwain's plans.

It wasn't all bad in Gainesville. The previous January, Grier was hanging out with a group of friends when he spotted a pretty coed. "Who is that?" he asked. She was Jeanne O'Neil, a former Tampa Bay Buccaneers cheerleader who had just transferred to Florida. Her first question was, "What position do you play?" Before long, they were inseparable and eventually married. In November 2016, as Grier sat out the season after transferring to

MOUNTAINEERS

West Virginia, their daughter Ellie was born.

With his senior season winding down Grier looked back at how far he had traveled from the vantage point of a perspective far different from that with which he had begun college. He now had two guides in his life: one his best friend and the other his daughter. "It's this deep love," he said. "It gives you perspective on life. . . . I'm just happy. I'm in a good spot."

Like Will Grier, your perspective goes a long way toward determining whether you slink through life amid despair, anger, and hopelessness or stride boldly through life with joy and hope. It's the difference between playing a game with vigor and determination or just going through the motions to get it over with.

Mary Magdalene is an excellent example. On that first Easter, she stood by Jesus' tomb crying, her heart broken, because she still viewed everything through the perspective of Jesus' death. But how her attitude, her heart, and her life changed when she saw the morning through the perspective of Jesus' resurrection.

So it is with life and death for all of us. You can't avoid death, but you can determine how you perceive it. Is it fearful, dark, fraught with peril and uncertainty? Or is it a simple little passageway to glory, the light, and loved ones, an elevator ride to paradise?

It's a matter of perspective that depends totally on whether or not you're standing by Jesus' side when it arrives.

[Having a family] gives you a new perspective on the way you live your life. It's not just you.

— *Will Grier*

**Whether death is your worst enemy or
a solicitous chauffeur is a matter of perspective.**

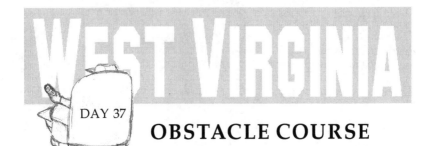

DAY 37

OBSTACLE COURSE

Read 2 Corinthians 12:23-33.

"I have been in prison more frequently, been flogged more severely, and been exposed to death again and again" (v. 23b).

Getting home turned out to be just as big an obstacle for the West Virginia women's basketball team as winning one of the biggest game in the program's history.

On their way to a 30-win season and the Big 12 co-championship, the tenth-ranked WVU women of 2013-14 traveled to Waco for a showdown with fifth-ranked Baylor on March 2. The Bears were riding a 35-game home win streak.

Baylor led 69-68 and had the ball as the final seconds ticked away. But juniors Linda Stepney and Crystal Leary trapped the Baylor ball handler and harried her into a wild throw. The ball went right into the hands of junior forward Averee Fields. With 12 seconds left, she took the ball the length of the floor for a layup. A late free throw put the 71-69 final on the scoreboard.

Thus did the West Virginia women lodge a landmark win that propelled them to their first regular-season conference title since 1992. Winning the game meant overcoming a huge obstacle. As it turned out, so did getting back home to Morgantown.

Waco was in the grips of an ice storm, so the team couldn't fly out. They took a bus ride to Austin, though that turned out to be quite an adventure in itself because of ice on the road. The 100-

mile drive took more than three hours.

In Austin, the Mountaineers learned they couldn't fly into Clarksburg because of a weather-related state of emergency there. So they flew into Pittsburgh, arriving around 11:30, but had to stay there for the night because of the road conditions.

Finally, everyone made it back to Morgantown Monday morning, just in time to begin practice for a Tuesday night game.

As a West Virginia team does in a game (and sometimes afterwards), we all face obstacles in life. They are those things that stand in the way of where we are and where we want to be or what we want to do. Some, such as physical problems, are not of our own making. Many of the barriers or roadblocks we face, however, are self-inflicted, a product of the poor choices we make.

We also face spiritual obstacles to our faith life. They keep us from getting where we want to be in our relationship with God. Unlike the privation and the suffering that Paul experienced, our spiritual obstacles are self-inflicted. They're the product of our sin or our indifference (itself a sin). Coldness seeps into our heart, and we allow a distance to grow between God and us, a distance that many of us have felt at one time or another.

What can we do? We remember that it wasn't God who put that obstacle in place; we must move, take action. We drop the sin and actively pursue that broken relationship. We turn back to God, open our hearts to him again, and kick that barrier down.

Sometimes [the] obstacles come after the success.
— Writer Mike Casazza on WVU's travails after beating Baylor

The only obstacles between God and us
are the ones we erect.

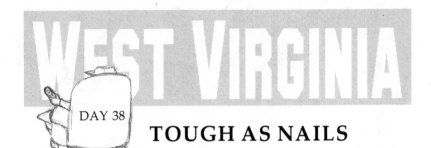

TOUGH AS NAILS

Read 2 Corinthians 11:21b-29.

"Besides everything else, I face daily the pressure of my concern for all the churches" (v. 28).

Skyler Howard took a shot to the ribs that sent him to the training room. When you're tough as nails and your team needs you, though, a simple thing like bruised ribs can't keep you out of the game.

Right before halftime of the 2016 season opener against the Missouri Tigers, Howard, WVU's "undersized" senior quarterback, wound up on the short and painful end of a busted play. He got "a shot to the rib cage that had them vibrating like [a] xylophone." He slowly returned to the backfield before looking to the sideline and going down in pain. A game that West Virginia had had under control was suddenly in doubt.

With backups in the game, WVU's last two possessions of the half resulted in turnovers and a Missouri field goal. WVU led 13-3 at the break, but without Howard, "the situation seemed dark."

It didn't get any brighter during halftime. Howard spent the intermission in the company of the training staff, undergoing X-rays to determine if he could play. The photographs were negative, but the ribs were still bruised. The team captain could play if he were tough enough to withstand the pain.

"Hey, I'm a ball player," Howard later said about going back into the game. Pain "is just football. Let's try it again."

MOUNTAINEERS

So he did. With Howard back on the field, the offense took the second-half kickoff and moved quickly to a touchdown. Rushel Shell broke off a 20-yard run, Howard completed passes of 22 and 24 yards, setting up a 1-yard touchdown run. The message was clear: The Tigers weren't going to win this game.

They didn't. Behind its tough quarterback, WVU won 26-11.

You don't have to be a Mountaineer quarterback to be tough. In America today, toughness isn't restricted to physical accomplishments and brute strength. Going to work every morning even when you feel bad, sticking by your rules for your children in a society that ridicules parental authority, making hard decisions about your aging parents' care often over their objections — you've got to be tough every day just to live honorably, decently, and justly.

Living faithfully requires toughness, too, though in America chances are you won't be imprisoned, stoned, or flogged this week for your faith as Paul was. Still, contemporary society exerts subtle, psychological, daily pressures on you to turn your back on your faith and your values. Popular culture promotes promiscuity, atheism, and gutter language; your children's schools have kicked God out; the corporate culture advocates amorality before the shrine of the almighty dollar.

You have to hang tough to keep the faith.

He's a tough kid. I don't think anybody in their right mind would question his toughness.
— *Dana Holgorsen on Skyler Howard*

**Life demands more than mere physical toughness;
you must be spiritually tough, too.**

DAY 39

THE REVOLUTIONARY

Read Matthew 3:1-12.

"After me will come one who is more powerful than I, . .
. . He will baptize you with the Holy Spirit and with fire"
(v. 11b).

West Virginia's head coach realized he had found his quarterback when he instigated a revolution in the huddle.

Fred Wyant has been called "one of the greatest quarterbacks in Mountaineer history." From 1952-55, his record as a starter was 30-4. He led the Mountaineers to the 1954 Sugar Bowl.

Wyant "was the only good player on his high-school team." His coach thus told his squad that Wyant was the only player allowed to carry the ball inside the 10-yard line. Eventually, the coach moved the demarcation line back to the 25 and then to midfield.

The team's dependence on their star quarterback reached its zenith in the final game of Wyant's senior year. His head coach told him, "Look, it's your last game and . . . if you want to carry [the ball] on every play, go ahead and do it." Wyant did.

WVU head coach Art Lewis didn't start Wyant in the 1952 season opener against Furman. The team played miserably, and finally with nine minutes left, Lewis told Wyant to go into the game. "I was fourth string and he put me in," Wyatt recalled.

The freshman quickly showed he was not awed by the situation. After three plays, the team was close to a first down. The coach motioned for his quarterback to punt the football.

Wyant turned back to the huddle and said, "I don't know about you guys but I don't want to kick the ball." As he recalled it, the huddle slowly came around. Wyant threw a long pass to Jack Stone for a touchdown.

When Wyant led WVU on another scoring drive and had them moving again when time ran out, Lewis had found his quarterback — despite his insubordinate revolution.

Throughout recorded history, revolutions on an obviously much grander scale than that of Fred Wyant's have changed the world. Revolutions from Russia to America have periodically swept across the world stage, demolishing the past in the process.

No revolution, however, has ever had an impact on history to match the one wrought by an itinerant preacher some two millennia ago. As God's prophet, John the Baptist saw it coming and preached it. This revolution was different in that what it sought was an end to rebellion. John's call was for repentance, a revolution of the soul, a change that would lead to living the way God has prescribed rather than rebelling against God's word.

This revolution shattered everything about human history in that for the first time God himself became a part of that history. The kingdom of heaven came to Earth in the person of Jesus Christ, a revolutionary such as the world had never seen before and will never see again.

It was like a light bulb went off.
— Fred Wyant on his teammates' reaction to his defiance of his coach

**All man-made revolutions pale beside the one
God wrought when he brought the Kingdom
of Heaven to Earth in Jesus.**

DAY 40

SOMETHING NEW

Read Ephesians 4:17-24.

*"You were taught . . . to put off your old self . . . and
to put on the new self, created to be like God in true
righteousness and holiness" (vv. 22, 24).*

Back when men's soccer was the new sport at WVU, the head
coach knew more about swimming, the field wasn't level, and the
players frequently visited the nearby woods during practice.

Soccer was formally introduced as the university's twelfth varsity sport in 1961. The new game in town started humbly with only
the most basic support from the athletic department. For instance,
Mountaineer swimming coach Lewis Ringer was appointed
the first head coach. He quickly gave way to Jim Markel, whose
experience was also in swimming. Markel "was a nice guy but he
didn't know a whole lot about soccer," recalled Martin Pushkin, a
goalkeeper on WVU's first team.

The facilities weren't exactly top-of-the-line either. A field on
the outskirts of town was the site for those early home matches. It
wasn't even level and was full of rocks. Ralph Rossi, a letterman
in 1964 and '65, said he could see only about half of the left side
because the field fell off so much. "The ball would roll down the
hill for a couple hundred yards once it rolled out of bounds," he
recalled.

The players had no rest room facilities available. If nature
issued a summons during practice, the guys ran over a hill and

MOUNTAINEERS

into the woods. What passed for a team locker room was in the old stadium; the players would dress there and then jog up Monongahela Boulevard to practice, a distance of about two miles.

Some of those pioneer players were international students who had played the game before. Some, however, were athletes from other sports simply trying to stay in shape. Pushkin, for instance, was a hurdler on the track team. "I got interested in soccer and I figured I could be a goalie. Why not?" he said. And so he was. "We took it seriously and we trained hard; we did the best that we could" with this new sport.

New things in our lives often have a life-changing effect. A new spouse. A new baby. A new job. A new sport at WVU. Something as mundane as a new HDTV can jolt us with change.

While new experiences, new people, and new toys may make our lives new, they can't make new lives for us. Inside, where it counts — down in the deepest recesses of our soul — we're still the same, no matter how desperately we may wish to change.

An inner restlessness drives us to seek escape from a life that is a monotonous routine. Such a mundane existence just isn't good enough for someone who is a child of God; it can't even be called living. We want more out of life; something's got to change.

The only hope for a new life lies in becoming a brand new man or woman. And that is possible only through Jesus Christ, he who can make all things new again.

We started off on a small scale.
— *WVU soccer pioneer Martin Pushkin*

A brand new you with the promise of a life worth living is waiting in Jesus Christ.

WEST VIRGINIA

YOU DECIDE

Read John 6:60-69.

"The words I have spoken to you are spirit and they are life. Yet there are some of you who do not believe" (vv. 63b-64a).

A spur-of-the-moment decision by Jim Carlen led directly to his first-ever defeat of the Pitt Panthers.

A pair of broken ankles permanently sidelined Ken Juskowich, a world-class soccer player who had scored the only goal for the United States in the 1963 Guatemalan Games. At the urging of WVU soccer coach Greg Myers, he tried out for the Mountaineer football team in 1966.

Juskowich recalled that it was toward the end of practice one day that the coaches agreed to give him a look. Returning kicker Carl "Chuck" Kinder was a senior, so they were willing to let just about anybody try a few field goals.

Juskowich kicked away for some 20 to 25 minutes when Carlen, the first-year head coach, walked over. "Son," he said, "I want you to get your stuff [from] wherever you are living on campus, because you are going to move into the dormitory and you're going to be on scholarship." Just like that, right in front of his players and coaches, Carlen had made a big decision about some-body who had never even played in a football game.

That decision paid big dividends in 1967. In the opener against Villanova, his first-ever game, Juskowich kicked four PATs and

MOUNTAINEERS

set a school record by booting four field goals in the 40-0 win.

That record didn't last long. On Oct. 7, the 3-1 Mountaineers hosted the Pitt Panthers in a game that was so dull many of the fans "were distracted by two attractive females playing tennis on the courts down below the field." Juskowich provided all the excitement; he broke his own record by kicking five field goals and scoring all the game's points in the 15-0 WVU win. The WVU defense held Pitt to -25 yards rushing and 21 yards total offense.

As with Jim Carlen's snap decision about Ken Juskowich and its effect on his football team, the decisions you have made along the way have shaped your life at every pivotal moment. Some decisions you made suddenly and carelessly; some you made carefully and deliberately; some were forced upon you. You may have discovered that some of those spur-of-the-moment decisions have turned out better than your carefully considered ones.

Of all your life's decisions, however, none is more important than one you cannot ignore: What have you done with Jesus? Even in his time, people chose to follow Jesus or to reject him, and nothing has changed; the decision must still be made and nobody can make it for you. Ignoring Jesus won't work either; that is, in fact, a decision, and neither he nor the consequences of your decision will go away.

Carefully considered or spontaneous — how you arrive at a decision for Jesus doesn't matter; all that matters is that you get there.

People don't make decisions like that anymore.
— Ken Juskowich on Jim Carlen's putting him on scholarship

A decision for Jesus may be spontaneous or considered; what counts is that you make it.

DAY 42

DEMOLITION MAN

Read Genesis 7.

"Every living thing on the face of the earth was wiped out" (v. 23a).

What WVU did to Clemson in the 2012 Orange Bowl wasn't just a beatdown. It was demolition, destruction, and devastation.

When the teams met in Miami on Jan. 4, few of the so-called "experts" gave WVU much of a chance. The game was give-and-take until one unforgettable defensive play in the second quarter. Trailing 21-17, Clemson drove to the Mountaineer 1-yard line. With a plunge into a heap of big bodies at the goal line, a Clemson player signaled touchdown. But safety Darwin Cook saw the ball come loose, grabbed it, and took off on a 99-yard jaunt.

The only thing that stopped Cook was Obie, the Orange Bowl mascot. Cook crossed the goal line and "gleefully leaped on mascot Obie, a smiling orange, and they both tumbled to the turf." Obie was unhurt by the collision. After the game, the two shared a hug as Cook said, "I didn't know you were a girl. I apologize."

Cook's play ignited the most spectacular scoring spree in bowl history. WVU scored five times in the second quarter to lead 49-20 at halftime. The destruction continued apace in the last half until the game mercifully ended with a shocking final score of 70-33. In wreaking all that havoc, West Virginia tied or broke eight separate team and individual bowl game records

ESPN's Heather Dinich wrote, "If you watched more than three quarters, you lasted longer than most of the Clemson fans [who] cleared out faster than a middle school during a fire drill."

"We just got outplayed, point-blank, period," admitted Clemson defensive end Andre Branch.

It was total destruction and demolition, pure and simple.

We've heard a lot across recent decades about "weapons of mass destruction." The phrase conjures up frightening images of entire cities and countries being laid to waste. The population is annihilated; buildings are flattened; the infrastructure is destroyed; air and water are polluted; foodstuff is rendered inedible.

While the hideous weapons that we have so zealously created can indeed wreak destruction, nothing we have can equal the weapon of mass destruction that is the wrath of God. Only once has its full fury been loosed upon his creation; the result was the mass destruction unleashed by the flood.

God has promised that he will never again destroy everything with water. When Christ returns, though, mass destruction of a particular kind will again lay waste the Earth.

Until then, as part of the ongoing battle between good and evil, we have the ultimate weapon of mass destruction at our disposal; it is our faith. With it, we play a vital part in what will be God's ultimate mass destruction: The total eradication of evil in the Day of our Lord.

Am I embarrassed? Definitely. I've never been a part of, never actually been on that side of getting beat like that.
— Clemson quarterback Tajh Boyd on the Orange Bowl

Our faith is a weapon of mass destruction, playing a key role in the eradication of evil.

DAY 43

IN GOD'S OWN TIME

Read James 5:7-12.

"Be patient, then, brothers, until the Lord's coming" (v. 7).

The Mountaineer coaches knew they had in hand a play that would score a go-ahead touchdown. They just needed to wait for the right time to call it.

West Virginia was 4-0 and was ranked seventh in the nation on Oct. 1, 1983, when the Pitt Panthers brought the nation's best college defense to Morgantown for a nationally televised game. Pitt led 21-17 in the fourth quarter before the Mountaineers put together a legendary game-winning drive.

After a punt and a penalty, WVU took possession at its own 10-yard line. Quarterback Jeff Hostetler calmly trotted into the huddle and told his team, "We've got 90 yards to go. Let's do it!"

The Mountaineers proceeded to do it by running right at that vaunted Pitt defense. Behind tight end Rob Bennett, tackles Brian Jozwiak (an All-America in 1985) and Kurt Kehl, guards Dave De-Jarnett and Scott Barrows, and center Bill Legg, the offense slugged its way across the ninety yards in fourteen plays, thirteen of them on the ground. And they did it between the tackles. Fullback Ron Wolfley carried four times for 31 yards, and running back Pat Randolph added 24 yards. The rest came from Hostetler.

Including the final six yards, which were set up by all of those inside runs. The Pitt defense drew in tighter with each run, and the coaches and Hostetler saw what was going on. The quarterback bootleg was wide open. "It was one of those things where you wait and you wait and you call it at the right time," Hostetler said. The right time came with the ball at the Panther 6.

Hostetler executed a perfect fake, and when the defense bit on the inside run, he went wide and scored untouched. He crossed the goal line, dropped to one knee, "and pointed toward the sky as the stadium exploded."

The waiting was over. WVU won 24-21.

Have you ever left a restaurant because the server didn't take your order quickly enough? Complained at your doctor's office about how long you had to wait? Wondered how much longer a sermon was going to last?

It isn't just the machinations of the world with which we're impatient; we want God to move at our pace, not his. For instance, how often have you prayed and expected — indeed, demanded — an immediate answer from God? And aren't Christians the world over impatient for the glorious day when Jesus will return and set everything right? We're in a hurry but God obviously isn't.

As rare as it seems to be, patience is nevertheless included among the likes of gentleness, humility, kindness, and compassion as attributes of a Christian.

God expects us to be patient. He knows what he's doing, he is in control, and his will shall be done. On his schedule, not ours.

We knew after pounding, pounding and pounding that it was there.
— Jeff Hostetler on the game-winning bootleg against Pitt

God moves in his own time, so often we must wait for him to act, remaining faithful and patient.

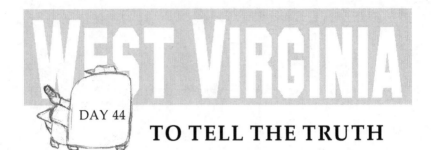
DAY 44

TO TELL THE TRUTH

Read Matthew 5:33-37.

"Simply let your 'Yes' be 'Yes,' and your 'No,' 'No';
anything beyond this comes from the evil one" (v. 37).

Wil Robinson thought they were telling the truth. As a team-mate reminded him, he should have remembered where he was.

From 1969-72, Robinson, an All-American point guard, set a number of school scoring records. Only Jerry West and Rod Hundley scored more points in their careers than Robinson did.

Robinson was a well-liked and popular player with a legion of fans among the WVU students. Not everyone knew who he was, though. School president James Harlow liked to get out among the students occasionally; he sometimes picked up student hitch-hikers. Robinson was once one of those.

As Robinson slid into the front seat of the president's car, Harlow asked him if he were a student. "No, sir," he replied. "I'm a basketball player. Who are you?" "I'm the president," Harlow answered. "Oh," was all the abashed Robinson could say.

Another humorous Robinson story took place in a game versus George Washington in 1970. With the score tied and the clock ticking down, coach Sonny Moran told his players to get the ball to Robinson. Then he turned to his point guard and told him to "let the clock run all the way down before you shoot it."

Sure enough, Robinson got the ball and dribbled some time away. But then he heard the George Washington students chanting: "Five, four, three." He frantically heaved up a shot that missed. Only then did he see the ten seconds still on the clock.

GW called timeout. "What were you doing, Wil?" a flabbergasted Moran asked. "I thought they were telling the truth," he replied. Forward Dick Symons piped up: "Will, this is Washington, D.C. Nobody tells the truth around here." (Robinson's shot with 22 seconds left in overtime won the game 92-91.)

Should Christians ever lie? Perhaps the more piercing question is "Can Christians lie to further what they believe to be the pursuit of good?" Jesus consistently admonishes us to tell the truth, and the Bible overwhelmingly condemns lying. Nevertheless, with the midwives in Exodus 1 and Rahab in Joshua 2, we have instances in which liars are not rebuked by God, but instead are blessed. That's because they lied to combat evil.

For most of us, our fabrications amount to little white lies. No, dear, that dress doesn't make you look overweight. No, officer, I wasn't speeding. Like so much of Christianity, what is in our heart when we lie (as we inevitably at some time will) determines whether we have earned God's displeasure.

Are we lying to strike against evil and injustice or to spare or ease another person's pain? Or are we lying out of our own self-serving interests to gain a worldly advantage? If it's the latter, we can be certain that we have sided with Satan, "the father of lies" (John 8:44), and not our Lord and Savior.

Trampling on the truth is as common as overpaid athletes and bad TV.
— *Former hockey coach Dan Bauer*

The nature of the temptation that leads us to lie determines whether we side with Satan or angels.

PROVE IT!

Read John 2:12-23.

"Then the Jews demanded of him, 'What miraculous sign can you show us to prove your authority?'" (v. 18)

The 2006 Sugar Bowl wasn't just another game for the Mountaineers; it was a chance to prove themselves. Man, did they ever!

Rich Rodriguez' fifth squad went 10-1 and won the program's third straight Big East championship. Despite all those wins, "the experts, the pundits, and even the fans were underwhelmed." That was largely because of the depleted conference the Mountaineers found themselves playing in through no fault of their own.

Miami, Virginia Tech, and Boston College had fled for greener pastures, leaving the Big East to be replaced by Connecticut, Cincinnati, South Florida, and Louisville. None of those programs could match the gridiron prowess of the schools that had left, so the Big East had a "bruised reputation." More than a few pundits argued the league was so weak it didn't merit a spot in the BCS.

The media also discounted West Virginia as being "too young, too small, and too underrecruited" to match up with their Sugar-Bowl opponent, the eighth-ranked and SEC-champion Georgia Bulldogs. The denigrating of the Mountaineers was so bad and so frequent the week of the game that UGA head coach Mark Richt got worried. "No one likes to hear they can't win or don't belong," he said.

He was right. With everything to prove and nothing to lose,

MOUNTAINEERS

the Mountaineers went out and played one of the greatest games in the school's history.

WVU bolted to a 28-0 lead by scoring on four straight possessions with two touchdowns from freshman running back Steve Slaton and two from sophomore wide receiver Darius Reynaud. Georgia rallied, and the game came down to Phil Brady's 10-yard gain on a fake punt at the Bulldog 48. The Mountaineers ran out the clock for the 38-35 win. They had nothing left to prove.

We, too, have to prove ourselves over and over again in our lives. To our teachers, our bosses or supervisors, that person we'd like to date, to our parents. We shouldn't be surprised at this; Jesus was constantly besieged by those seeking a sign through which he would prove himself to them.

For us, it's always the same question: "Am I good enough?" And yet, when it comes down to the most crucial situation in our lives, the answer is always a decisive and resounding "No!" Are we good enough to measure up to God? To deserve our salvation? Absolutely not; we never will be. That's why God sent Jesus to us.

The notion that only "good" people can be church members is a perversion of Jesus' entire ministry. Nobody is good enough — without Jesus. Everybody is good enough — with Jesus. That's not because of anything we have done for God, but because of what he has done for us. We have nothing to prove to God.

It may have been the best thing to happen to them.
— Mike Casazza on the disrespect WVU received before the Sugar Bowl

> **The bad news is we can't prove to God's**
> **satisfaction how good we are; the good news**
> **is that because of Jesus we don't have to.**

DAY 46

THE GREATEST

Read Mark 9:33-37.

"If anyone wants to be first, he must be the very last, and the servant of all" (v. 35).

More than a quarter century after it happened, it's still considered by many fans to be the greatest play in the greatest season in WVU football history. And it was a busted play.

When 7-0 WVU hosted Penn State on Oct. 29, 1988, the Mountaineers needed a win to change the perception that they couldn't beat the Nittany Lions. Not coincidentally, a win would keep the Mountaineers' hopes for a slot in the BCS title game alive.

Legendary WVU quarterback Major Harris was a sophomore that season. Years later he recalled, "We're playing on national television, . . . we were already ranked higher [than Penn State], but there was this sense that we were the underdogs."

From the start, though, there was also a sense "that not only was WVU going to win this game, . . . but they were going to dominate in doing so." They did, jumping out to a 41-8 halftime lead and thrashing the Nittany Lions 51-30. Harris once described that game as "the apex of my career" and beating Penn State to be "tops for me." So was the almost mythical run he pulled off.

It came in the first half. Hurrying his team to the line to beat the play clock, Harris couldn't remember the play head coach Don Nehlen had sent in and he had called. He knew it was an option but not the direction right or left. He guessed wrong.

MOUNTAINEERS

Harris turned right; the rest of the team went left. Writer Tara Curtis described what happened: "He faked out the entire Penn State team leaving no less than seven tacklers grabbing air on the way to the most gorgeous touchdown run in school history." Secondary coach Dave Lockwood called Harris' play "one of the greatest runs I have ever seen in college football history."

The run was a mere 26 yards and it didn't win the game, but it still resonates with WVU fans as the greatest play ever.

We all want to be the greatest. The goal for the Mountaineers and their fans in every sport is the Big 12 title with a shot at the national crown. The competition at work is to be the most productive sales person on the staff or the Teacher of the Year. In other words, we define being the greatest in terms of the struggle for personal success. It's nothing new; Jesus' disciples saw greatness in the same way.

As Jesus illustrated, though, greatness in the Kingdom of God has nothing to do with the secular world's understanding of success. Rather, the greatest are those who channel their ambition toward the furtherance of Christ's kingdom through love and service, rather than their own advancement. This is, obviously, a complete reversal of status and values as the world sees them.

But who could be greater than the person who has Jesus for a brother and God for a father? And that's every one of us.

'My fault, coach.' 'I think I can live with it.'
— Major Harris-Don Nehlen exchange after the Penn State run

**To be great for God has nothing to do
with personal advancement and everything to do
with the advancement of Christ's kingdom.**

DAY 47

THE HARD WAY

Read Matthew 7:7-14.

"But small is the gate and narrow the road that leads to life, and only a few find it" (v. 29).

Rasul Douglas' path to college football stardom was so hard that it sometimes included not having enough to eat.

As a WVU senior in 2016, Douglas, a cornerback, tied for the national lead with eight interceptions. He was first-team All-Big 12 and a Walter Camp second-team All-America. *ESPN* named him the Big 12 Defensive Player of the Year. In January 2017, Dana Holgorsen bestowed the same honor on him for the Mountaineers. The Eagles took him in the third round of the 2017 NFL draft.

That success didn't come easy. Douglas grew up in a neighborhood where, as he put it, "kids are lost to the streets." But he had "a strong-willed grandmother, a little league coach who saw something special in him and an innate passion to play sports."

Douglas didn't catch the attention of the big-time football programs out of high school. When Nassau Community College offered him a chance to play, his coach convinced Douglas to give it a try. It wasn't easy.

Nassau didn't have dorms. Douglas found an apartment eight miles from the campus. He didn't have a car, so he had to take a bus every to day to class and to practice. Because his grandmother was raising his six siblings, he was on his own financially.

He had so little money that he struggled to pay for food. Often, he waited until the evening to eat his lone meal of the day. Other times, he went to McDonald's and bought a hamburger off the value menu. He would eat half of the burger for lunch and save the rest for dinner.

But as West Virginia defensive coordinator Tony Gibson said, Douglas is "just a kid that keeps fighting." So he did "the juco grind"; he went to class, practice, and study hall and did the work. On the field, he became a star, and WVU came calling in 2015.

Is it hard to get into Heaven? Well, yes and no.

Becoming a Christian is literally as easy as ABC. Admit that you are a sinner, that you have done, said, and thought things that offended God. Believe that Jesus Christ is the way to heal that breach between God and you. Confess your faith in Jesus as your Lord and Savior. Easy enough.

For all too many, though, finding salvation is remarkably hard. Jesus said as much, declaring the entrance to heaven to be a small gate with a narrow roadway. Why? The simple, awful truth is that too many people aren't willing to believe Jesus' literal words about the narrow gate. They fall prey to the world's relativistic viewpoint, kick Jesus to the curb, and decree that any way to Heaven is just as good as another.

There's only one problem with that: It won't work. Jesus said he is "the" way, and not "a" way. The forgiving and healing power of faith in Jesus Christ is the only way to get into Heaven.

That was probably the hardest part of my life, for sure.
— *Rasul Douglas on his time at Nassau Community College*

Too many people miss out on Heaven because following Jesus turns out to be too hard for them.

LIKE CLOCKWORK

Read Matthew 25:1-13.

"Keep watch, because you do not know the day or the hour" (v. 13).

For all the world, it looked as though the Mountaineers had a heartbreaking loss. That was right before they wound up with a scintillating win. It was all a matter of time.

Sophomore guard Jevon Carter, who led the Mountaineers with 26 points, said, "It was like a movie" that unfolded in slow motion. The movie was the final seconds of the semifinals of the 2016 Big 12 men's basketball tournament. For Carter and his WVU teammates, the flick had all the makings of a horror show.

What Carter saw was Oklahoma star Buddy Hield get the ball, take a couple of dribbles across half court, and heave a shot that banked through the basket at the buzzer. Hield and the Oklahoma faithful celebrated a buzzer-beater that had propelled the sixth-ranked Sooners to a 70-69 win over ninth-ranked WVU.

"Championship game, main character makes the last shot. So when he made that I was like, 'Is this possible?'" Carter said in the locker room as he continued his movie motif.

Senior guard Jaysean Paige, who won the conference's Sixth Man Award, hit a jumper with 11.2 seconds on the clock that gave WVU a 68-67 lead. After OU missed a layup, the Sooners fouled with 1.8 seconds to play. Senior forward Jonathan Holton hit one of two free throws for a 69-67 lead. Hield had one last chance, and he made the most of it.

Or so it seemed at least for a few minutes. As soon as he saw the replay, though, Carter knew otherwise. "Nah, that didn't count," he confidently said. "They're going to give the game to us."

And how could that happen? After the buzzer sounded, the referees gathered around a monitor to review Hield's shot. A few tense moments passed before they ruled the ball had left Hield's hand a fraction of a second too late. He had run out of time, and the buzzer had beaten him.

WVU had a 70-69 win and was on to the tournament finals.

We may pride ourselves on our time management, but the truth is that we don't manage time; it manages us. Hurried and harried, we live by schedules that seem to have too much what and too little when. By setting the bedside alarm at night, we even let the clock determine how much down time we get. A life of leisure actually means one in which time is of no importance.

Every second of our life — all the time we have — is a gift from God, who dreamed up time in the first place. We would do well, therefore, to consider what God considers to be good time management. After all, Jesus himself warned us against mismanaging the time we have. From God's point of view, using our time wisely means being prepared at every moment for Jesus' return, which will occur — well, only time will tell when.

Time wasn't on my side, I guess.
   — OU's Buddy Hield after his game-winning shot was waved off

**We mismanage our time when we fail
to prepare for Jesus' return even though
we don't know when that will be.**

LIVE ACTION

Read James 2:14-26.

"Faith by itself, if it is not accompanied by action, is dead"
(v. 17).

The pre-game banter was literally trash talk, but West Virginia's play sure wasn't trashy.

"Did he really say that?" That was the reaction around the WVU football program when, shortly before the Pitt game of 1961, a Panther player declared that West Virginia was "rebuilding with Western Pennsylvania garbage." In the player's defense, he didn't expect the remark to show up in the papers, but it did.

Needless to say, the WVU coaches made sure their players — especially the guys from Western Pennsylvania — saw the quote. "I remember when that article came out because [head coach Gene Corum] talked about it, but I was never garbage!" recalled one of those Western Penn guys, tight end Ken Herock, who went on to a pro career.

Pitt may have done the talking, but once the game started it was the Mountaineers who did the playing. They marched 74 yards in 17 plays on their opening possession and led 7-6 at halftime.

They then wrapped the game up with a pair of touchdowns in the third quarter from halfback Roger Holdinsky. The first score came on a 30-yard pass from quarterback Fred "Colt 45" Colvard. The second TD came on a 31-yard sweep around right end. Holdinsky thus became the first WVU player to score two touchdowns against Pitt since Nick Nardacci did it in 1923.

The team also gained some revenge on the mouthy Pitt player, running at him all afternoon with multiple blockers. Late in the game, after the player was slow to get up, halfback Eli Kosanovich got in a little trash talking of his own. He stood over the Panther and taunted, "If we're garbage, then what are you guys?"

After the 20-6 win, the WVU players openly joked about the unfortunate garbage quote. Halfback Jim Procopio chanted, "We are the garbage boys — you can't beat the garbage men!" And on this day, he was right.

Talk is cheap. Consider your neighbor or coworker who talks without saying anything, who makes promises she doesn't keep, who brags about his own exploits, who can always tell you how to do something but never shows up for the work. You know that speech without action just doesn't cut it.

That principle applies in the life of a person of faith too. Merely declaring our faith isn't enough, however sincere we may be. It is putting our faith into action that shouts to the world of the depth of our commitment to Christ.

Even Jesus didn't just talk, though he certainly did his share of preaching and teaching. Rather, his ministry was a virtual whirlwind of activity. As he did, so are we to change the world by doing. Anybody can talk about Jesus, but it is when we act for him that we demonstrate how much we love him.

Jesus Christ is alive; so should our faith in him be.

Whoa, ammo!
— Assistant coach Russ Crane's response to the 'garbage' comment

Faith that does not reveal itself in action is dead.

DAY 50

WILD AND CRAZY

Read Mark 3:1-12.

"John's clothes were made of camel's hair, and he had a leather belt around his waist. His food was locusts and wild honey" (v. 4).

The 2012 Baylor game was one wild and crazy affair.

The final score says it all: West Virginia 70 Baylor 63. And this was football, not basketball, a game in which the team that wound up on the short end of the score truly didn't lose so much as simply ran out of time.

Pretty much everything about this game was wild and crazy. Mountaineer quarterback Geno Smith threw more touchdowns (eight) than incompletions (six). The game set an NCAA record for the most points scored involving ranked teams. The teams combined to score seventy points in the first half, one field goal shy of the all-time NCAA record.

The wild and crazy shootout produced a number of team and conference offensive records. The most dubious record belonged to Baylor: most points scored by a losing team. The oddest record belonged to WVU's All-American junior wide receiver Stedman Bailey: shortest time holding a conference record. During the game, he set a Big 12 record with 314 yards receiving. Later in the game, a Baylor receiver broke it.

Smith's 47-yard completion to Bailey set up Andrew Buie's short touchdown run for a 56-35 WVU lead in the third quarter.

MOUNTAINEERS

Baylor responded with a pair of touchdowns, but then Bailey scored on TD catches of 87 and 39 yards. (Bailey set a WVU record with five touchdown catches.) Baylor got within seven with 3:08 left and then literally ran out of time. Dustin Garrison ran for 17 yards to convert a third down, and WVU ran out the clock.

"Not every Big 12 game is like this, " WVU's head man Dana Holgorsen said. No, they're not; they're not this wild and crazy.

Part of the lure of sports is how the games sometimes lapse into the wild and crazy, like the WVU-Baylor scorefest But ponder a moment the notion that Jesus calls each one of us to a wild, crazy, and adventuresome life, though perhaps not one as bizarre as that of John the Baptist. If this is true, then why is it that church and faith life quite often seem so boring to many of us? Why don't Christians lead lives of adventure and excitement?

Many do. Heading into the uncharted waters of the mission field is certainly exciting. Helping the homeless turn their lives around isn't dull at all. Neither is working with youth, teaching Sunday school, entering the chaplaincy for the military, or riding with a Christian biker gang.

The truth is too many of us play it safe. We prefer to do what we want to do rather than what God calls us to do. As a result, we pass on the chance for our lives to be a great adventure story. We may just be common, ordinary folks, but if we truly follow Jesus, there is nothing common or ordinary about our lives.

I might need more gun powder for this game.
— Jon Kimble, WVU's Mountaineer mascot, at the 2012 Baylor game

We are a bunch of wild and crazy guys and gals
when we truly surrender our lives to Jesus.

DAY 51

WITHOUT FAIL

Read Luke 22:54-62.

"Peter remembered the word the Lord had spoken to him: 'Before the rooster crows today, you will disown me three times.' And he went outside and wept bitterly" (vv. 61b-62).

The campaign to pay for newly built Mountaineer Field was such a failure that the state legislature finally had to step in.

Into the 1920s, West Virginia's football and baseball teams played their games on the Athletic Field, which is now the location of Mountainlair Plaza. A first-ever bowl game following an undefeated season in 1922 spurred unprecedented interest in the football program. Athletic director Harry Stansbury decided to take advantage of the fan support.

With a seating capacity of about 12,000, the Athletic Field had outgrown its usefulness. The university's governing board gave Stansbury permission to solicit funds for a new stadium along Falling Run. The site was chosen because of its proximity to the railroad stations, the primary means of travel at the time.

Stansbury wanted a facility that would seat about 35,000. The cost was driven up some by the location, which required that a stream that emptied into the Monongahela River be diverted.

The plan was to finance the construction using private funds. A Stadium Corporation was formed that came up with the ambitious plan of raising $500,000 in 15 minutes at a home football game against Washington & Jefferson in 1923. Unfortunately, the weather was cold and wet and WVU lost the game. The effort was a failure; only about $100,000 was raised.

A second campaign was initiated statewide to make up the difference, but it, too, fell far short of what was needed. Ticket sales couldn't make up the shortfall, so by the mid-1930s, the debt with interest on the stadium was still nearly $500,000.

Finally, in 1935, the state legislature bailed out the athletic department and its failed fundraising by paying off the balance.

Failure is usually defined by expectations, like WVU's plans to raise $500,000. A baseball player who hits .300 is a star, but he fails seventy percent of the time. We grumble about a postal system that manages to deliver 500 million items each day.

And we are often our own harshest critics, beating ourselves up for our failings because we expected better. Never mind that our expectations were unrealistic to begin with.

The bad news about life is that failure — unlike success — is inevitable. Only one man walked this earth perfectly and we're not him. The good news about life, however, is that failure isn't permanent. In life, we always have time to reverse our failures as did Peter, he who failed our Lord so abjectly.

The same cannot be said of death. In death we eternally suffer the consequences of our failure to follow that one perfect man.

It took more than 30 years for the legislature to consider another big-ticket facility project.
— John Antonik on the aftermath of the failed stadium fundraising

**Only one failure in life dooms us to eternal failure
in death: failing to follow Jesus Christ.**

DAY 52

THE PRIZE

Read Philippians 3:10-16.

"I press on toward the goal to win the prize for which God has called me heavenward in Christ Jesus" (v. 14).

Rod Thorn once garnered an honor no other WVU athlete has ever received or is ever likely to.

A guard, Thorn completed his All-American career in Morgantown in 1963 third on the school's all-time scoring list behind Jerry West and Hot Rod Hundley. He was never a secret. "By the time [he] had reached high school, there were very few basketball fans in the state who didn't know who he was."

Thorn's dad, Joe, was a former minor league pitcher in the St. Louis Cardinals' farm system. He started working with his son when he was 4 years old. Before Rod's hands were big enough to hold a basketball, his father had him use a volleyball. Rod started playing organized basketball when he was 6 years old, touring with some older kids on a team called the Rinky Dinks.

Thorn took naturally to baseball. "I could hit curve balls when I was six or seven years old because [his dad] threw them to me all of the time," he said. Despite his excellence at basketball, the younger Thorn was set on following in his father's footsteps as a professional baseball player and was a star in the Southern Conference at WVU. In his senior year, though, he was knocked unconscious when he was hit in the back of the head by a baseball. That put an end to his career on the diamond.

MOUNTAINEERS

By Thorn's senior year of high school, he had received letters from just about every major school in the country. He narrowed his choices to Duke and West Virginia. The West Virginia legislature decided to put a little extra pressure on Thorn. The legislators declared him a "natural resource," a less than subtle way of begging him to stay in the state.

Whether the honor helped or not, Thorn, of course, opted to play for the Mountaineers.

Even the most modest and self-effacing among us can't help but be pleased by prizes and honors. Such recognition symbolizes the approval and appreciation of others, whether it's an Employee of the Month plaque, an award for sales achievement, or the sign declaring yours to be the neighborhood's prettiest yard.

Such prizes and awards are often the culmination of the intentional pursuit of personal achievement and accomplishment. They represent accolades and recognition from the world. Nothing is inherently wrong with any of that just as long as we keep those honors in perspective.

That is, we must never let awards become such idols that we worship or lower our sight from the greatest prize of all and the only one truly worth winning. It's one that won't rust, collect dust, or leave us wondering why we worked so hard to win it in the first place. The ultimate prize is eternal life, and it's ours through Jesus Christ.

What in the world is this [legislature] thinking about?
— Rod Thorn's reaction to being named a 'natural resource'

**God has the greatest prize of all
ready to hand to you through Jesus Christ.**

DAY 53

GOOD LUCK

Read Acts 1:15-25.

*"Then they prayed, 'Lord, you know everyone's heart.
Show us which of these two you have chosen.' . . . Then
they cast lots" (vv. 24, 25a).*

Did the Mountaineers have a little luck on their side in their
defeat of Georgia Tech in the 2007 Gator Bowl? Perhaps.

If WVU had any luck in the first half of the game of Jan. 1,
it was all bad. All-American running back Steve Slaton pulled
himself out of the game in the second quarter with a deep thigh
bruise. Pat White, the Big East's all-time leading rusher for a quarterback, re-injured his left ankle, hurt his neck, and banged up
his throwing hand. Fullback Owen Schmitt said that at halftime,
"Pat came into the locker room [with] six bags [of ice] on him. His
hand was the size of a grapefruit."

Meanwhile, Tech scored on four straight possessions in the
first half to jump out to a 28-3 lead. Even after WVU rallied to
make it 28-17 at the break, Tech got a lucky bounce on an onside
kick to start the second half and scored in four plays. 35-17.

But then the ball started bouncing WVU's way, and the Mountaineers took advantage to score 21 points in only seven minutes
of the third quarter. Consider:

1) WVU scored when All-American center Dan Mozes snapped
the ball when he sensed Tech was offsides. On a "freeze play,"
none of the linemen moved. White hit receiver Tito Gonzales for

a 57-yard touchdown. WVU declined the penalty. (Duh!) 35-24.

2) A sack by safety Charles Pugh gave the beleaguered WVU defense a key stop. The offense went on a 7-play drive with White hitting wide receiver Brandon Myles for a 14-yard score. 35-31.

3) Pat McAfee shanked the kickoff, but the ball bounced off two Tech players before WVU safety John Holmes fell on it. Two plays later, White ran it in from the 15. With help from a lucky bounce or two, WVU suddenly led 38-35. That was the final score.

Ever think sometimes that other people have all the luck? Some guy wins a lottery while you can't get a raise of a few lousy bucks at work. The football takes a lucky bounce the other team's way and WVU loses a game. If you have any luck to speak of, it's bad.

To ascribe anything that happens in life to blind luck, however, is to believe that random chance controls everything. But here's the truth: Luck exists only as a makeshift explanation for something beyond our ken. Even when the apostles in effect flipped a coin to pick the new guy, they acknowledged that the lots merely revealed to them a decision God had already made.

It's true that we can't explain why some people skate merrily through life while others suffer in horrifying ways. We don't know why good things happen to bad people and vice versa. But none of it results from luck, unless, as the disciples did, you want to attribute that name to the force that does indeed control the universe; you know — the one more commonly called God.

The stadium was bumping. Everything seemed to be clicking.
— Pat McAfee on WVU's run of good luck in the third quarter

A force does exist that is in charge of your life,
but it isn't luck; it's God.

WEST VIRGINIA

DAY 54

KEEP OUT!

Read Exodus 26:31-35; 30:1-10.

"The curtain will separate the Holy Place from the Most Holy Place" (v. 26:33).

West Virginia couldn't get into the club, and thus the destiny of Mountaineer athletics was forever altered.

WVU was a member of the 17-member Southern Conference in 1953 when representatives from seven of the league's strongest schools decided to break away and form what is now the ACC. The proposed new league immediately cast about for an eighth member. West Virginia seemed the logical choice.

"I really think [the ACC] is where we belonged," said Pete White, a center for the 1954-55 Mountaineer basketball teams. "It's who we had played all along." The defection left the Mountaineers in a gutted conference that certainly wasn't big-time. The opponents would be the likes of Davidson, Furman, VMI, and Richmond.

So WVU athletic director Roy "Legs" Hawley worked tirelessly to land that eighth spot in the ACC. The Associated Press reported that West Virginia "definitely was being considered," primarily because of the school's "basketball prowess" "in spite of travel and schedule difficulties involved."

That geography, however, ultimately may have swung the vote against the school. In December, the seven members met again and decided to accept Virginia, which was then competing as an independent. Tony Constantine of the *Morgantown Post*

MOUNTAINEERS

bluntly said, "The geography is being blamed again . . . for West Virginia's exclusion from the rebel faction. . . . We're too far away from the rest of the schools."

"Those lengthy trips on mostly two-lane roads" thus altered WVU's sports history, keeping the school from orienting itself more toward the South and sending it casting about for a home. The school stayed in the Southern Conference through 1967 and then was independent until 1990. It aligned itself with the Big East until casting its fate westward with the Big 12 in 2012.

That civic club with its membership by invitation only. The sky boxes at sporting events reserved for a precious few. That neighborhood with the homes boasting price tags equal to some small countries' GNP. We know all about being shut out of some club, some group, some place. "Exclusive" is the word.

The Hebrew people, too, knew about not being granted access to an exclusive place or group. Only the priests could come into the presence of the holy and survive. Then along came Jesus to kick that barrier down and give us direct access to God.

In the process, though, Jesus created another exclusive club; its members are his followers, Christians, those who believe he is the Son of God and the savior of the world. This club, though, extends a membership invitation to everyone in the whole wide world; no one is excluded. Whether you're in or out depends on your response to Jesus, not on arbitrary gatekeepers.

I really think that the difficulty in getting into Morgantown hurt us.
— WVU's Pete White on being excluded from the new ACC

**Christianity is an exclusive club, but an invitation
is extended to everyone and no one is denied entry.**

WEST VIRGINIA

DAY 55

THE INTERVIEW

Read Romans 14:1-12.

"We will all stand before God's judgment seat. . . . So then, each of us will give an account of himself to God" (vv. 10, 12).

The interview process Don Nehlen went through to land the West Virginia job was, as he put it, "nothing short of weird."

The quarterbacks coach at Michigan, Nehlen had just returned from a recruiting trip after the 1979 season when Bo Schembechler called him into his office. He told him that Dick Martin, WVU's athletic director, had called and was interested in him. "I wasn't aware that there was an open job at West Virginia," Nehlen said.

When he finally did talk to Martin, they agreed to meet at the Pittsburgh airport. They hit it off until the meeting took a weird turn. As they watched, a reporter from a Pittsburgh TV station broke the news that Martin was hiring a new football coach. The reporter gave two names; neither one of them was Nehlen.

Nehlen's response was an angry outburst. It included a declaration that he wasn't sure he was interested in the WVU job and ended with, "I don't have time to come here for this."

Martin insisted the story wasn't true. Two days later, he called Nehlen and they met again, this time at a hotel near the airport. Again, it didn't turn out as Nehlen expected. When the door to the room was opened, he saw Martin and ten other people.

Nehlen was dressed for recruiting, not for a formal meeting

with an athletic board. He also hadn't even brought a resume. Upset again with Martin, he plunged right in and told them how it would be if they hired him. He did all the talking; the board members didn't even ask any questions; they just listened.

The weirdness wasn't over. Nehlen stayed in a high school rectory that night; not even his wife knew he was there. One of the priests knocked on his door and told him he had a phone call. It was Martin. The athletic council had said of Nehlen, "He's it."

You probably know a thing or two about job interviews. If so, you've experienced the stress and the anxiety that are part of any interview. You tried to appear calm and relaxed while struggling to come up with reasonably original answers to banal questions and to hide your opinion that the interviewer was a total geek.

We all will undergo one final interview on God's great Judgment Day when we must give an accounting of ourselves. John 5:22-23 declares that God has committed all judgment to Jesus, a startling instance of one of the New Testament's most consistent themes: the Father and the Son are one.

In our final interview, Jesus will judge each of us according to the rules laid out by God the Father. All eternity will be at stake and a resume of good deeds, sterling accomplishments, and unblemished grade-point averages won't help. The only way to ace this one is to have Jesus know who you are through your faith in him.

I was a little spooked and wondering how anybody knew I was there.
— Don Nehlen on the phone call he got at the rectory from Dick Martin

**In our final interview, Jesus will judge us using
God's criteria, the first of which is faith in the Son.**

DAY 56

WORK ETHIC

Read Matthew 9:35-38.

*"Then he said to his disciples, 'The harvest is plentiful but
the workers are few. Ask the Lord of the harvest, therefore,
to send out workers into his harvest field'" (vv. 37-38).*

Joe Alexander became a first-round pick in the NBA draft the
old-fashioned way: He worked for it.

After drawing limited interest from lower-division colleges,
Alexander walked on at West Virginia in the fall of 2005. He saw
little action that season, but WVU coaches and players quickly
learned that Alexander's "work habits bordered on compulsion."

For instance, one night the power went out in the Coliseum.
Determined to work out, Alexander drove his Nissan through the
facility's tunnel and used its headlights to create enough light to
shoot some baskets.

He spent so much time at the Coliseum that he began finding
places where he could keep his stuff. Point guard Joe Mazzulla
recalled the time he wanted to listen to his CD player in the locker
room but didn't have any batteries. Alexander told him to hold
on, disappeared behind some bleachers, and returned in a few
minutes with a couple of brand new batteries.

Alexander moved into the starting lineup his sophomore season, but his production tailed off so badly the last half that his
"basketball career was barely surviving." It received a major jolt
when Bob Huggins was named the head coach after the 2006-07

season. That's because Huggins emphasized weight training and strength. That gave Alexander a new way to work, and he tackled it with his usual enthusiasm.

He gained twenty pounds with increased stamina before the 2007-08 season started, and he had a breakout year. The Mountaineers went 26-11 and advanced to the Sweet 16. Alexander led the team in scoring and rebounding and was named to the first-team All-Big East squad.

He then opted to turn pro and became the first WVU player since Ron Williams in 1968 to be taken in the NBA's first round.

Do you embrace hard work or try to avoid it? No matter how hard you may try, you really can't escape hard work. Funny thing about all these labor-saving devices like cell phones and laptop computers: You're working longer and harder than ever. For many of us, our work defines us perhaps more than any other aspect of our lives. But there's a workforce you're a part of that doesn't show up in any Labor Department statistics or any IRS records.

You're part of God's staff; God has a specific job that only you can do for him. It's often referred to as a "calling," but it amounts to your serving God where there is a need in the way that best suits your God-given abilities and talents.

You should stand ready to work for God all the time, 24-7. Those are awful hours, but the benefits are out of this world.

I've always believed that if you put in the work, the results will come.
— *Michael Jordan*

God calls you to work for him using the talents and gifts he gave you; whether you're a worker or a malingerer is up to you.

DAY 57

LANGUAGE BARRIER

Read Mark 16:9-20.

"Go into all the world and preach the good news to all creation" (v. 13).

Language problems once resulted in an encounter between an exuberant Mountaineer fan and a police officer's billy club.

Dudley Sargent DeGroot headed up the WVU football program for two seasons (1948-49). He may well be the only coach in history — perhaps in any sport — to have a master's degree in oology, the study of birds' eggs. His two-year record in Morgantown was 13-9-1, but dissension among the players in '49 was so bad it made the papers. He resigned two weeks after the season ended.

His successor was Art Lewis, a "burly, bushy-browed, mountain of a man," who let toughness determine his starters. At practice, he lined players up in a one-on-one drill, and the survivor was the starter. Lewis led the Mountaineers to five Southern Conference championships and 58 wins from 1950-59. His '53 team went to the Sugar Bowl, the school's first-ever trip to a major bowl.

The 1952 squad manhandled Pitt 16-0 behind a defense led by sophomore guard Gene Lamone that limited the Panthers to 161 total yards. The jubilant players carried Lewis off the field and all the way to the shower.

The game was played in Pittsburgh. Aware of what might happen, a Pitt official told a West Virginia delegation before the kickoff that "the goal posts were theirs if they won." Said that same official after the game, "They took us at our word alright."

As the clock wound down, WVU fans went after those goal posts. A police supervisor told an officer to "let them have it," but that officer didn't understand the reference was to the goal posts. He let one of the fans have it all right — with his billy club.

The unfortunate Mountaineer fan's encounter with the billy club illustrates a common problem: Even when we speak the same language, we often don't communicate well enough to prevent misunderstanding. Recall your overseas vacation or your call to a tech support number when you got someone who spoke English but didn't understand it. Talking loud and waving your hands doesn't facilitate communication; it just makes you look weird.

Like many other aspects of life, faith has its jargon that can sometimes hinder understanding. Sanctification, justification, salvation, Advent, Communion with its symbolism of eating flesh and drinking blood: These and many other words have specific meanings to Christians that may be incomprehensible, confusing, and downright daunting to the newcomer or the seeker.

But the heart of Christianity's message centers on words that require no explanation: words such as hope, joy, love, purpose, and community. Their meanings are universal because people the world over seek them in their lives. Nobody speaks that language better than Jesus.

The well-lubricated West Virginia fan never felt a thing.
— John Antonik after a police officer 'let him have it'

Jesus speaks across all language barriers
because his message of hope and meaning
resounds with people everywhere.

FAMILY TRADITIONS

Read Mark 7:1-13.

*"You have let go of the commands of God and are holding
on to the traditions of men" (v. 8).*

From some carpet to a cheer and chant requiring coordination
and manual dexterity, WVU athletics has its own enduring and
endearing traditions.

A unique WVU tradition was begun by the students. It's the
"First Down Cheer," which is heard and performed during home
games prior to the announcement of a Mountaineer first down.
Fans raise their hands and cheer in unison until the first down
call is made. Then they lift their arms up and down three times,
clap, and signal to the end zone while chanting "first down."

Head basketball coach Fred Schaus (1954-60) enjoyed a little
showmanship. In 1955, a WVU fan and supporter suggested to
the coach that he have his team run out on a gold and blue carpet
during player introductions. Schaus liked the idea. The tradition
was discontinued for a while, but "rolling out the carpet" has
been a Mountaineer staple at home games since 1978. It begins
when the Coliseum's public address announcer exclaims, "Let's
roll out the carpet and greet the Mountaineers!"

One tradition virtually guaranteed to choke up every true-blue
Mountaineer fan is the singing by the team and the fans of "Take
Me Home, Country Roads" after a win at home. The song has
been played at every pre-game show since 1972.

MOUNTAINEERS

Then there's the Mountaineer Mantrip, "a nod to the state's proud coal industry and heritage." WVU fans line a path along which the football team walks to enter the stadium. The walk is named after the shuttle that transports miners into an underground mine at the start of their shift.

You encounter traditions practically everywhere in your life. WVU sure has them. So does your workplace. Your family may have a particular way of decorating the Christmas tree, or it may gather to celebrate Easter at a certain family member's home.

Your church undoubtedly has traditions also. A particular type of music, for instance. Or how often you celebrate Communion. Or the order of worship.

Jesus knew all about religious tradition; after all, he grew up in the Church. He understood, though, the danger that lay in allowing tradition to become a religion in and of itself, and in his encounter with the Pharisees, Jesus rebuked them for just that.

Jesus changed everything that the world had ever known about faith. This included the traditions that had gradually arisen to define the way the Jews of his day worshipped. Jesus declared that those who truly worship God do not do so by simply observing various traditions, but rather by establishing a meaningful, deep-seated personal relationship with him.

Tradition in our faith life is useful only when it helps to draw us closer to God.

The post game: it's a bit of a tear jerker.
    — Writer Eric Herter on singing 'Country Roads' after a win

Religious tradition has value only when it serves to strengthen our relationship with God.

ALL IN

Read Mark 12:28-34.

"Love the Lord your God with all your heart and with all your soul and with all your mind and with all your strength" (v. 30).

After the game's final play, "the entire West Virginia sideline spilled onto the field, hooting and hollering." Thus did the Mountaineers demonstrate the same enthusiasm and zeal with which they played the game.

A season that would conclude with perhaps the greatest single-game performance in WVU history (See Devotion No. 42.) was on the line in Cincinnati on Nov. 12, 2011. In their last season in the Big East before heading to the Big 12, the Mountaineers needed to win out to claim the league title and the BCS berth. They were only 3-2 in conference play and had no wiggle room.

Head coach Dana Holgorsen had no explanation for what were called a pair of "head-scratching loss[es]." He did, however, have a message when he addressed his team before it took on Cincinnati: Play with energy, play with excitement, play for each other. He also delivered that message during his weekly news conference when he threatened to take only 55 players to Cincinnati if they "did not pick themselves up and learn how to fight."

The message hit home. When the defense put together a goal-line stand, quarterback Geno Smith and receiver Stedman Bailey ran onto the field to congratulate their teammates. Throughout the game, the players lifted each other up during the inevitable times of adversity

A 23-yard pass to Tavon Austin on third-and-15 set up a 1-yard touchdown run by Shawne Alston. With 8:52 left, WVU led 24-21.

With three seconds left, Cincinnati lined up for a 31-yard field goal to send the game into overtime. Safety Eain Smith blocked it. The result? "One word," Geno Smith said. "Pandemonium. "

That's just what happens when a bunch of enthusiastic Mountaineers celebrates a big win.

What fills your life, your heart, and your soul so much that you sometimes just can't help what you do? We all have zeal and enthusiasm for something, whether it's WVU football, sports cars, our family, scuba diving, or stamp collecting.

But do we have a zeal for the Lord? We may well jump up and down, scream, holler, even cry — generally making a spectacle of ourselves — when West Virginia scores. Yet on Sunday morning, if we go to church at all, we probably sit there showing about as much enthusiasm as we would for a root canal or an IRS audit.

Of all the divine rules, regulations, and commandments we find in the Bible, Jesus made it crystal clear which one is number one: We are to love God with everything we have. All our heart, all our soul, all our mind, all our strength.

If we do that, our zeal and enthusiasm will burst forth. Like the Mountaineers, we just won't be able to help ourselves.

The energy was great. It was great all over the sideline.
— Stedman Bailey on the enthusiasm at the Cincinnati game

**The enthusiasm with which we worship God
reveals the depth of our relationship with him.**

DAY 60

THE MOTHER LODE

Read John 19:25-30.

"Near the cross of Jesus stood his mother" (v. 25).

WVU women's soccer coach Nikki Izzo-Brown called Amanda Hill "one of the most competitive women I've ever met." Part of Hill's drive came from her wish to make her mother proud.

From 2012-15, Hill started every single game at midfielder for West Virginia. In 2015, she was a second-team All-American and a first-team Academic All-American. She was twice second team All-Big Twelve. During her four seasons, the Mountaineers went 62-14-12 and won four straight Big Twelve championships.

Hill's competitive drive was forged by her mother, Lori. Basketball, hockey, lacrosse, and soccer: she excelled at them all, in part because she had to. Her mother would never let her quit what she started. That even applied to cross country. "I'm not really sure why I signed up to run for fun," Amanda said.

Lori was a single mom who worked the midnight shift at a local hospital and slept while Lori and her brother, Dan, were at school. That left her ready to take them to whatever practices or games they had in the afternoon and evenings.

As Amanda put it, her mother "didn't have much other time for her own things once we came along. Herself wasn't a concern."

About that cross country. It changed Amanda's life tragically. She was 12 when she took fifth place among almost 200 runners. Her mother and she then headed home for a soccer game.

MOUNTAINEERS

Brother Dan, a decade older than Amanda, and his girlfriend were on their way to a friend's wedding when they crested a hill and saw an SUV on its side. His girlfriend recognized the mangled car before he did: It was Lori's. Amanda survived the crash but her mother did not.

Doctors said it would take Amanda five weeks to get back on the soccer field. She was playing in three. Why was she in such a hurry? "I couldn't wait to get back out on that field and get back after it," she said. "Just [to] make her proud."

Like Lori Hill, mamas often sacrifice their personal happiness and time for their children. No mother in history, though, has faced a challenge to match that of Mary, whom God chose to be the mother of Jesus. Like mamas and their children throughout time, Mary experienced both joy and perplexity in her relationship with her son.

To the end, though, Mary stood by her boy. She followed him all the way to his execution, an act of love and bravery since Jesus was condemned as an enemy of the Roman Empire.

But just as mothers like Lori Hill — and perhaps yours — would apparently do anything for their children, so will God do anything out of love for his children. After all, that was God on the cross at the foot of which Mary stood, and he was dying for you, one of his children.

I feel like I know what she wants me to do, so I just do that.
— Amanda Hill on how her mother still guides her life

**Mamas often sacrifice for their children,
but God, too, will do anything out of love
for his children, including dying on a cross.**

DAY 61

CHEAP TRICKS

Read Acts 19:11-20.

"The evil spirit answered them, 'Jesus I know, and I know about Paul, but who are you?'" (v. 15)

WVU head football coach Sol Metzger used a sneaky trick involving a local car salesman to keep the player who has been called "the greatest all-around athlete in Mountaineer history."

Hired in 1914, Metzger launched an aggressive recruiting effort that yielded Ira Errett Rodgers. He had played four years of football at Bethany College but as a prep school player because there was no high school near his home.

At WVU, Rodgers was the sole team captain in basketball, football, and baseball as a senior in 1919. He lettered four times in all three sports. In 1919, he led the nation in scoring and was WVU's first consensus All-American football player. His career total of 313 points stood as a school record for sixty years until All-American placekicker Paul Woodside broke it.

A fullback, Rodgers was not only a shifty runner, but he could "throw the football like a baseball, hard and accurate . . . 50 yards or more." As a result of his talent, WVU "revolutionized football tactics by demonstrating what a powerful weapon the forward pass" could be. Legendary sportswriter Grantland Rice wrote, "There may be a better all-round football player in America than Rodgers of West Virginia, but no one has uncovered his name."

But Metzger had to resort to trickery to keep Rodgers around.

MOUNTAINEERS

As the 1915 season neared, other schools tried everything they could to get to Rodgers and persuade him to leave WVU. The Pitt coaches, for instance, were convinced they could lure Rodgers away if they could only talk to him. One scout from a rival school came to Morgantown and managed to abscond with the star. Only he left with Paul Vance, a local car salesman who had agreed to impersonate Rodgers and allow himself to be kidnapped.

Scam artists are everywhere — and they love trick plays. An e-mail encourages you to send money to some foreign country to get rich. That guy at your front door offers to resurface your driveway at a ridiculously low price. A TV ad promises a pill to help you lose weight without diet or exercise.

You've been around; you check things out before deciding. The same approach is necessary with spiritual matters, too, because false religions and bogus Christian denominations abound. The key is what any group does with Jesus. Is he the son of God, the ruler of the universe, and the only way to salvation? If not, then what the group espouses is something other than the true Word of God.

The good news about Jesus does indeed sound too good to be true, but the only catch is that there is no catch. When it comes to salvation through Jesus Christ, there's no trick lurking in the fine print. There's just the truth, right there for you to see.

Paul Vance allowed himself to be lured away by the [rival] school for a couple of days until he was discovered not to be Ira Rodgers.
— John Antonik on Sol Metzger's trick

God's promises through Jesus sound too good to be true, but the only catch is that there is no catch.

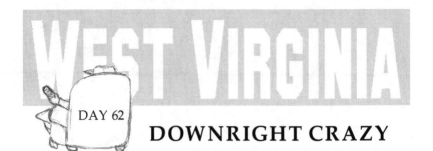

DAY 62

DOWNRIGHT CRAZY

Read Luke 13:31-35.

"Some Pharisees came to Jesus and said to him, 'Leave this place and go somewhere else. Herod wants to kill you.' He replied, 'Go tell that fox . . . I must keep going today and tomorrow and the next day'" (vv. 31-33).

What coach would do a crazy thing like telling the press — which, of course, his players heard — that his team didn't stand a chance before proceeding to list the reasons why? Don Nehlen did, and it helped WVU pull one of its most stirring upsets ever.

The Mountaineers opened the 1982 season against mighty Oklahoma and its wishbone in Norman. In the spring, Nehlen warned his players not to believe anything they read in the newspapers. He then went out and said publicly that the heat would wilt his team and that the game was a mismatch that shouldn't even be played. "They'll kill us," he declared.

However, he privately told his players something even crazier than what he was telling the public: that the heat wouldn't bother them, that if they could go into the game at halftime less than ten points down, they would win the game in the fourth quarter.

Sure enough, the Sooners jumped on the Mountaineers early. Nehlen kept urging his team not to get flustered. They didn't. Making his first start, quarterback Jeff Hostetler repeatedly sent receiver Darrell Miller in motion and hit him with little passes, and Oklahoma was confused by it. WVU led 20-14 at the half.

MOUNTAINEERS

The locker room was an absolute madhouse since everything the coach had been telling them — and not the press — was coming true. "They were going crazy," Nehlen said of his players. He tried to remind them they still had a half to play, but "they were certain that they were going to win."

They did. In the fourth quarter, they popped a 45-yard draw play with leading rusher Curlin Beck for a 41-27 lead. Tied into its wishbone, OU couldn't throw the ball. With time running out, they were giving the ball to the fullback. The 41-27 score stood up.

Nehlen and his crazy strategy had worked.

What some see as crazy often is shrewd instead. Like the time you went into business for yourself or when you decided to go back to school. Maybe it was when you fixed up that old house. Or when you bought that new company's stock.

You know a good thing when you see it but are also shrewd enough to spot something that's downright crazy. Jesus was that way too. He knew that his entering Jerusalem was in complete defiance of all apparent reason and logic since a whole bunch of folks who wanted to kill him were waiting for him there.

Nevertheless, he went because he also knew that when the great drama had played out he would defeat not only his personal enemies but the most fearsome enemy of all: death itself.

It was, after all, a shrewd move that provided the way to your salvation.

I'm going to try to set a smokescreen for the folks in Oklahoma.
— Don Nehlen to his players on his crazy strategy vs. OU

It's so good it sounds crazy — but it's not: through faith in Jesus, you can have eternal life with God.

CLUELESS

Read Matthew 16:21-23.

"[Y]ou do not have in mind the things of God, but the things of men" (v. 23b).

For a good while, Kevin White, Jr., was pretty much clueless. When he got it, though, he really got it.

White didn't get serious about football until his senior year of high school when he made the move from defensive back to wide receiver. As he clued in on football, though, he remained clueless about his grades. They were so bad he couldn't qualify for a major college scholarship, so he wound up at a junior college in 2010. He was still clueless. He failed to turn in his paperwork for his courses one semester and then didn't fill out his financial aid forms. He couldn't even suit up for a junior college team.

All along, though, White had been training at a facility catching balls fired out of machines and completing speed, strength, and agility exercises. Even as he had jeopardized his football career with his cluelessness and talked about doing social work for a living, White started to get it. He began to take his training and his football seriously.

Each evening he trekked to a nearby soccer field and hurled footballs with his two brothers and Devon Blake, his best friend and teammate. Blake recalled that one evening at dusk it was snowing and his fingers started to "feel like freeze pops." White made them all stick around another hour until he was satisfied.

MOUNTAINEERS

"Some guys will mature in the classroom, some on the field, and some in their social life. [White] matured in all of them at the same time," said White's junior college coach, Mark Duda.

Clued in now, White wound up at WVU in 2013 because it was close to home and he liked the offense. As a senior in 2014, he was third in the nation with 109 receptions, first-team All-Big 12, and second-team All-America. He was taken in the 2015 NFL draft.

Clueless. Suffice it to say, it's not a compliment. It's an interesting word in that it is its own oxymoron. People are clueless only when they do indeed have the clues at hand and still don't get it. It's not to be confused with ignorance, which occurs when people don't have access to facts, figures, and information.

From the desert-dwelling Israelites grumbling about Moses and God to the Pharisees and other religious leaders of Jesus' day, the Bible is replete with the clueless. Simon Peter, who had all the clues he needed standing right in front of his face, drew a soul-searing rebuke from Jesus for being clueless.

The Bible remains relevant today because centuries after it was compiled, human nature is still the same. As it was in Jesus' time, people who have heard the Gospel may still be divided into the clued in and the clueless: those who get it and those who don't. Fortunately for the clueless, they can always change groups as Peter did. They can affirm Jesus as their savior and surrender their lives to him. They just need you to clue them in.

I just made up my mind and said I'm gonna make it happen.
— Kevin White, Jr., clueing in on football while in junior college

**Clueless or clued in is a matter of whether
you have given your life to Jesus.**

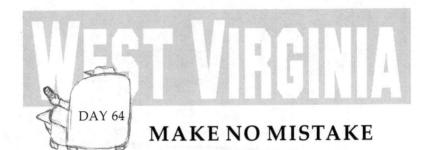

DAY 64

MAKE NO MISTAKE

Read Mark 14:66-72.

*"Then Peter remembered the word Jesus had spoken to
him: 'Before the rooster crows twice you will disown me
three times.' And he broke down and wept" (v. 72).*

Coach Bob Huggins' mistake wound up bailing WVU out and
clinching a win in the NCAA Tournament.

On March 20, 2015, the 23-9 Mountaineers met the 23-9 Bulls of
Buffalo in the opening round of the Big Dance. The score was tied
at 62 as the clock ticked away the final three minutes. Sophomore
forward Devin Williams hit a pair of free throws to ease WVU
into the lead. Each team then missed a shot before Williams con-
trolled the ball and called timeout after a wild scrum.

Buffalo's strategy at this point was simple: Play good defense,
force the Mountaineers into a bad shot, and then hold the ball for
the final shot to tie or win it. It worked perfectly — almost. The
Bulls' defense kept WVU from a good shot with the game clock
ticking toward thirty seconds and the shot clock about to hit zero.

All-Big 12 point guard Juwan Staten penetrated and looked
for anyone he could find open for a shot. That turned out to be
sophomore guard Tarik Phillip. With 28 seconds to play, Phillip
buried a three, the ball settling into the net as the shot clock
buzzed. That killed Buffalo's chances, and the Mountaineers
went on to win 68-62 and advance to the next round.

But it was all a mistake. Had Huggins remembered he was

there, Phillip wouldn't have been on the floor at all. He had been inserted into the lineup for his defense and his rebounding. He was not in the game to shoot.

During the timeout, Huggins had intended to replace Phillip with a shooter. In all the excitement and tension, he simply forgot. "It wasn't for him to take the shot," the head coach said.

A mistake led directly to one of the game's key plays.

It's distressing but it's true: Like WVU coaches and players and Simon Peter, we all make mistakes. Only one perfect man ever walked on this earth, and no one of us is he. Some mistakes are just dumb. Like locking yourself out of your home or walking facefirst into a sliding glass door.

Other mistakes are more significant and carry with them the potential for devastation. Like heading down a path to addiction. Committing a crime. Walking out on a spouse and the children.

All these mistakes, however, from the momentarily annoying to the life-altering tragic, share one aspect: They can all be forgiven in Christ. Other folks may not forgive us; we may not even forgive ourselves. But God will forgive us when we call upon him in Jesus' name.

Thus, the twofold fatal mistake we can make is ignoring the fact that we will die one day and subsequently ignoring the fact that Jesus is the only way to shun Hell and enter Heaven. We absolutely must get this one right.

My absentmindedness probably won the game.
— Bob Huggins on the win over Buffalo

Only one mistake we make sends us to Hell
when we die: ignoring Jesus while we live.

A BETTER PLACE

Read Hebrews 11:13-16.

"They were longing for a better country — a heavenly one" (v. 16a).

Owen Schmitt believed he belonged in a better place. He did; it turned out to be Morgantown.

Schmitt was "a very good high school player, but [was] not good enough to end up in a big program with a free ride." So he settled on a Division III school. He settled but he didn't accept. Schmitt believed he was a better player than that.

He made some calls, but nothing worked. Maryland told him to stay where he was and become an All-American. WVU was constantly on his mind because he had some friends playing in Morgantown. So one December afternoon in 2003, Schmitt and his mother showed up at the Puskar Center with a box of VHS tapes. He told the coaches he was looking for a place to play.

Head coach Rich Rodriquez liked everything he saw. Schmitt joined the team in the spring of 2004 as a walk-on. He had found his better place, and WVU fans are still grateful.

After a year on the scout team, Schmitt was not only on scholarship in the fall of 2005 but was the starting fullback. With quarterback Pat White at the helm, Schmitt and halfback Steve Slaton made one of the best rushing tandems in the country. Before the 2006 season, the trio was featured on the cover of *Sports Illustrated*'s regional article "Big Men on Campus."

MOUNTAINEERS

As a senior in 2007, Schmitt "was arguably one of the best fullbacks in the nation." He was tagged the "Runaway Beer Truck" for his physical style, which let him set one WVU record that is not likely to be broken. In his three years, Schmitt broke eleven facemasks, about one in every three games he played.

He had found a better place indeed. WVU lost only five times during Schmitt's three seasons. His teams won the Sugar Bowl, the Gator Bowl, and the Fiesta Bowl, a run of bowl success unprecedented in West Virginia football history.

America is a nation of nomads, packing up the U-Haul and the car and moving on the average about once every five years. We move because like Owen Schmitt we're always seeking something better. Better schools for the kids. A job with better career opportunities. Better weather.

We're seeking that better place that will make our lives better. Quite often, though, we wind up in a place or in circumstances that are just different, not better. So we try again.

God is very aware of this deep longing in our hearts for something better than what we have now. As only he can, he has made provision for it. What God has prepared for us, however, isn't a place that's just better, but rather a place that is perfect. He has also thoughtfully provided clear directions about how to get there, though we won't get any help from our GPS.

Jesus is the way to that place, that perfect place called Heaven.

He couldn't shake the feeling he was capable of doing so much more.
— Writer Mike Casazza on Owen Schmitt's desire for a better place

**God knows our deep longing for a better place,
so he has prepared one for us: Heaven.**

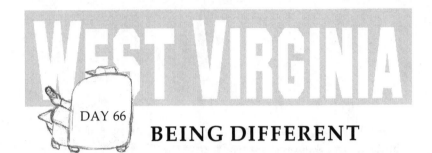

DAY 66

BEING DIFFERENT

Read Daniel 3.

*"We want you to know, O king, that we will not serve
your gods or worship the image of gold you have set up"*
(v. 18).

One of football's enduring stereotypes is that of the punter or
placekicker who is different. Flaky, if you will. West Virginia's
Todd Sauerbrun certainly fit the bill.

Sauerbrun has been called "one of the greatest special teams
players to come through Morgantown" and "arguably the best
punter in school history." He was All-America as a senior in 1994
and a three-time All-Big East selection. His '94 punting average
of 48.4 yards per punt was an NCAA record.

Sauerbrun kicked to the beat of his own drummer. Quarterback Chad Johnston laughingly recalled his saying he came to
West Virginia because the team was "good enough to go to bowl
games but the offense was always bad enough for him to kick a
lot." Somehow he learned the phone number of the press box; he
would often call after games to check on his punting average.

One day at practice, Mountaineer head coach Don Nehlen
wanted to get in some situational kicking work with Sauerbrun.
He blew his whistle and yelled for his punter. No answer. Another
blast of the whistle again yielded only silence. Finally, one of the
players looked toward the training table at the bowl end of the
stadium. There was Sauerbrun loading up his plate with food.

Nehlen burst out laughing and ended practice right then.

Nehlen had a strict rule that players had to wear a sport coat for the team dinner the night before a game. One time Sauerbrun forgot his jacket, and Nehlen stopped him. "Give me some money and I'll go to the Burger King," the punter suggested. Nehlen dug into his trousers and turned his pockets inside out. "Todd, I'm the West Virginia football coach," he said. "I don't have any money."

WVU's "different" punter told that story a lot.

While we live in a secular society that constantly pressures us to conform to its principles and values, we serve a risen Christ who calls us to be different. Therein lies the great conflict of the Christian life in contemporary America.

But how many of us really consider that even in our secular society we struggle to conform? We are all geeks in a sense. We can never truly conform because we were not created by God to live in such a sin-filled world in the first place. Thus, when Christ calls us to be different by following and espousing Christian beliefs, principles, and practices, he is summoning us to the lifestyle we were born for.

The most important step in being different for Jesus is realizing and admitting what we really are: We are children of God; we are Christians. Only secondarily are we citizens of a secular world. That world both scorns and disdains us for being different; Jesus both praises and loves us for it.

That was just Todd.

— *Chad Johnston on Sauerbrun's flaky behavior*

The lifestyle Jesus calls us to is different from that of the world, but it is the way we were born to live.

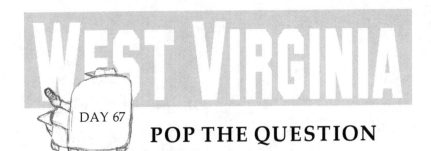

DAY 67

POP THE QUESTION

Read Matthew 16:13-17.

"'But what about you?' he asked. 'Who do you say I am?'" (v. 15)

The Mountaineers desperately needed their All-American halfback. Turns out all they had to do was ask.

Nick Nardacci was a three-year starter from 1922-24, playing on West Virginia teams that went 25-2-2, including the undefeated powerhouse of 1922. He was named a second-team All-America along with guard Joe Setron following that 1922 season. (Tackle Russ Meredith was a first-team All-America that storied season.)

Nardacci's head coach was Clarence "Fats" Spears, who stood 5-9 and topped the scales at nearly 300 pounds. The rotund coach was always sensitive about his weight.

He also had a quick temper. In the 1921 game against Lehigh, he was disturbed by a uniformed policeman who kept walking up and down the Mountaineer sideline. Several times he asked the man to leave and was rebuffed. Finally, Spears grabbed the cop, hoisted him into the air, and threw him over a fence.

As a senior in 1924, Nardacci was the undisputed star of the team that christened old Mountaineer Field with an undefeated season at home. With one game left in the season against favored Washington & Jefferson, Nardacci suddenly quit the team, citing the need to concentrate on his medical school studies.

As Spears and assistant coach Ira Rodgers prepared for the

game, each evening the head coach invariably said, "Now if we just had Nardacci." Finally, Rodgers said to his boss, "If you think you need Nardacci so much, why don't you call him up and ask him to come back to the team?"

Spears did and Nardacci did. Behind what was called "one of the greatest games of [Nardacci's] career," WVU upset W&J 40-7.

Life is an ongoing search for answers. Thus, whether our lives are lived richly or are wasted is largely determined by both the quality and the quantity of the answers we find. What's for dinner? Where are we going on vacation? What kind of team will West Virginia have this season?

But we also continuously seek answers to questions at another, more crucial level. What will I do with my life? Why am I here? Why does God allow suffering and tragedy?

An aspect of wisdom is reconciling ourselves to and being comfortable with the fact that we will never know all the answers. Equally wise is the realization that the answers to life's more momentous questions lie within us, not beyond us.

One question overrides all others; it's the one Jesus asked of Peter: "Who do you say I am?" Peter gave the one and only correct answer: "You are the Son of the Living God." How we answer that question is really the only one that matters, since it decides not just how we spend our lives but how we spend eternity.

I'm like most coaches now, standing on the sideline hoping somebody asks him a question.

— Bobby Bowden

**Only one question in life determines
our eternal fate: Who do we say Jesus is?**

THE PIONEER SPIRIT

Read Luke 5:1-11.

"So they pulled their boats up on shore, left everything and followed him" (v. 11).

One player thought a press meant you couldn't move. Another that if you hit the backboard the shot wasn't any good. But they were among the pioneers of women's basketball at WVU.

Today, West Virginia's women practice their basketball in a $24.1 million practice facility and play their games in the 14,000-seat Coliseum. Through 2017-18, they have won at least twenty games in twelve of the last fifteen seasons and have made twelve trips to the NCAA Tournament. The 2016-17 squad won the Big Twelve Tournament, beating second-ranked Baylor in the finals.

It hasn't always been quite that glorious, though. Back in 1973, athletic director Leland Byrd told Kittie Blakemore, an instructor in the school's PE department, she was the coach of the first-ever women's team. He handed her the keys to a university van and a ten-game schedule against local colleges.

Blakemore's biggest challenge was talent: There wasn't much of it because girls basketball was new in the state. When Blakemore went to the first-ever West Virginia high school state tournament, her reaction was, "Oh, my, I've got to recruit *these* girls!"

Thirty-seven players tried out for the first team, but only a few actually knew anything about playing the game. (See above for the backboard and the press defense.)

MOUNTAINEERS

Blakemore, assistant Barbara Walker, and trainer Diane Nolan managed to assemble a squad of fifteen players good enough to play. One quit before the first-ever game, played on Jan. 16, 1974, against West Liberty. The team uniforms hadn't arrived yet, so the players wore "pinnies," a vest-like jersey that tied at the waist. The record shows the pioneers won that first game 59-55. Leslie Sergy had 18 points and Sara Roberts scored eleven.

Women's basketball had arrived at WVU.

Going to a place in your life you've never been before requires a willingness to take risks and face uncertainty head-on. You may have never helped start a new sports program at a major college, but you've had your moments when your latent pioneer spirit manifested itself. That time you changed careers, ran a marathon, learned Spanish, or went back to school.

Attempting new things invariably begets apprehension; on the other hand, when life becomes too comfortable and too much of a routine, it gets boring. The same is true of God, who is downright dangerous because he calls us to be anything but comfortable as we serve him. He summons us to continuously blaze new trails in our faith life, to follow him no matter what. Stepping out on faith is risky all right, but the reward is a life of accomplishment, adventure, and joy that cannot be equaled anywhere else.

[Girls high school] basketball had just started in West Virginia, so the girls really didn't know much about the game.
— *Kittie Blakemore on beginning WVU women's basketball*

Unsafe and downright dangerous, God calls us out of the place where we are comfortable to a life of adventure and trailblazing in his name.

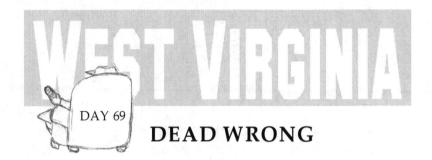

DAY 69

DEAD WRONG

Read Matthew 26:14-16; 27:1-10.

"When Judas, who had betrayed him, saw that Jesus was condemned, he was seized with remorse" (v. 27:3).

Don Nehlen was quite upset when he saw what a booster did at a fundraiser. Boy, did he have it all wrong.

After Nehlen was hired as the WVU head football coach in 1979, West Virginia Governor Jay Rockefeller asked him how much money he needed to finish the stadium then under construction. Nehlen said they needed a million dollars to build a first-class facility. So Rockefeller invited him to a dinner at the governor's mansion with some of the university's wealthiest boosters.

After everyone had eaten, the governor explained they were there to raise a million dollars to provide WVU's new head football coach with what he needed to build a winning program. He started the ball rolling by writing a personal check for $125,000. Then Rockefeller had an aide pass out 3x5 cards. "Write down what you think you can give," he said. "When we're up to a million, you can go home. If we don't get a million, nobody leaves."

Nehlen was sitting next to a man named Orville Thomas. The new head coach was amazed to see Thomas write down $80,000 on his card. "To me, $80,000 was unbelievable," Nehlen said. But then to the coach's dismay, when the aide came around to pick up the cards, Thomas tucked his away in his coat pocket.

Once the cards were totaled up, the aide said, "We're close, but we have to up it some." So they passed the cards around again.

Now Nehlen was really chagrined. They would have reached the million-dollar goal if Thomas had just turned his card in.

This time, Thomas handed in his card. When the cards were totaled, the aide announced, "Governor, we've got it. It's just over a million." Thomas then learned over to Nehlen and said conspiratorially, "I got you $80,000 extra, didn't I?" Nehlen had had what the booster was up to all wrong.

There's wrong, there's dead wrong, and there's Judas wrong. We've all been wrong in our lives, but we can at least honestly ease our conscience by telling ourselves we'll never be as wrong as Judas was. A close examination of Judas' actions, however, reveals that we can indeed replicate in our own lives the mistake Judas made that drove him to suicidal despair.

Judas ultimately regretted his betrayal of our Lord, but his sorrow and remorse, however boundless, could not save him. His attempt to undo his initial wrong was futile because he tried to fix everything himself rather than turning to God in repentance and begging for mercy.

While we can't literally betray Jesus to his enemies as Judas did, we can match Judas' failure in our own lives by not turning to God in Jesus' name and asking for forgiveness for our sins. In that case, we ultimately will be as dead wrong as Judas was.

Gosh dang it, if this guy would have turned his card in, we'd have had enough.
— Don Nehlen, initially wrong about Orville Thomas' card trick

**A sin is the first wrong; failing to ask God
for forgiveness of it is the second.**

DAY 70

PAY YOUR RESPECTS

Read Mark 8:31-38.

*"He then began to teach them that the Son of Man must
suffer many things and be rejected by the elders, chief
priests and teachers of the law, and that he must be killed"*
(v. 31).

The Mountaineers failed to get the respect they felt they had
earned. A defeat of fourth-ranked Miami took care of that.

As the weeks of the 1993 football season rolled along, two
things could be counted on each weekend: The Mountaineers
would win and they would get more ticked off. That's because
the team just didn't get much respect.

There they were, boasting a gaudy 9-0 record on their way to
an undefeated regular season. There they were also, the nation's
lowest-ranked undefeated team at No. 9.

Part of the problem was the schedule. Oh, the lineup sounded
good: defeats of Maryland, Missouri, Virginia Tech, Louisville,
Pittsburgh, and Syracuse. It just didn't look good; the combined
record of WVU's nine victims was a dismal 17-47-1.

Thus, the nationally televised Miami game of Nov. 20 would
clue the country in about the Mountaineers. The Canes showed
up 8-1 and ranked No. 4. Because they were so respected, they
were still in the hunt for the national title. WVU took care of that.

The Mountaineers stood toe to toe with Miami and led most of
the last half. Early in the fourth quarter, though, the Canes took

the lead at 14-10. With 7:30 to go, WVU fashioned its answer.

Mike Baker's punt return set the offense up at the Miami 30. Two plays later, tailback Robert Walker, on his way to his sixth straight 100-yard rushing game, erupted through a hole opened up by All-American tackle Rich Braham. Fullback Rodney Woodard took out two linebackers, and Walker scored from the 19.

The defense stood its ground, and the offense ran out the clock for the 17-14 win. Duly respected, the Mountaineers jumped to No. 3 the following week in the *USA Today/CNN* poll.

Rodney Dangerfield made a good living with a comedic repertoire that was basically only countless variations on one punch line: "I don't get no respect." Dangerfield was successful because he struck a chord with his audience. Like the late comedian, we all seek a measure of respect in our lives. We want the respect, the esteem, and the regard we feel we have earned.

But more often than not we don't get it. Still, we shouldn't feel too badly; we're in good company. In the ultimate example of disrespect, Jesus — the Son of God — was treated as the worst type of criminal. He was arrested, bound, scorned, ridiculed, spit upon, tortured, condemned, and executed.

God allowed his son to undergo such treatment because of his high regard and his love for each one of us. We are respected by almighty God! Could anyone else's respect really matter?

For nine weeks, we got no respect.
— Robert Walker after the '93 Miami game

You may not get the respect you deserve,
but at least nobody's spitting on you
and driving nails into you as they did to Jesus.

DAY 71

QUITE AN IMPRESSION

Read Mark 6:1-6.

"And [Jesus] was amazed at their lack of faith" (v. 6).

Coach Don Nehlen wanted his team to make an impression. What resulted was one of college football's most iconic helmets.

Nehlen took over the WVU football program in December 1979. He started out by watching game film to see what kind of team he had and ran into a problem: The uniforms and helmets were so plain he had trouble telling which team was West Virginia. Nehlen told equipment manager Mike Kerin he wanted "a dark, blue helmet, and I want a WV on both sides."

At a trade show in Chicago, Kerin met with a decal company and asked for ideas for a logo. The designs he got back were all duds. In Morgantown, Sports Information Director Mike Parsons was in something of a panic. He was putting together the 1980 football media guide. Before they could print it, they needed the new logo for the cover. Only it obviously didn't exist yet.

Over the years, neither Nehlen, Kerin, or Parsons could agree on the exact particulars that led to the new logo's design. They all, however, acknowledged John Martin, a renowned graphic artist and illustrator who lived in Kansas. His brother, Dick, was WVU's athletic director at the time.

The decision was made to get Martin involved. He spent a few days playing around with some ideas. The one he preferred came to be known as the Flying WV; it was born on a sheet of wax

MOUNTAINEERS

paper. His inspiration was mountains. "When you put a W and a V together, you had mountains," he said.

Back home, Mountaineer officials knew they had a hit as soon as they saw it. The Flying WV made its first appearance in the 1980 media guide. It soon became the link between the team and the fan base and caught on like crazy.

Today, the Flying WV continues to make an impression as one of the most identifiable logos in the country.

You bought that convertible mainly to show off; a white sedan would transport you more efficiently. You seek out subtle but effective ways to gain the boss' approval. You may be all grown up now, but you still want your parents' favor. You dress professionally but strikingly and take your prospective clients to that overpriced steak house.

In our lives we are constantly seeking to impress someone so they'll remember us and respond favorably to us. That's exactly the impression we should be making upon Jesus because in God's scheme for salvation, only the good opinion of Jesus Christ matters. On the day when we stand before God, our fate for eternity rests upon Jesus remembering and responding favorably to us.

We don't want to be like the folks in Jesus' hometown. Oh, they impressed him all right: with their lack of faith in him. This is not the impression we want to make.

I wanted a distinct helmet.
— Don Nehlen on the impetus for the creation of the Flying WV

Jesus is the only one worth impressing,
and it is the depth of your faith — or the lack of it
— that impresses him.

MEMORY LOSS

Read 1 Corinthians 11:17-29.

"[D]o this in remembrance of me" (v. 24).

The 2009-2010 season is one of the most memorable campaigns in WVU men's basketball history.

For starters, the team went 31-7, a school record for wins. It advanced to the Final Four for the first time since the 1959 squad made it to the championship game. The team finished in the top ten for the first time since the 1960-61 bunch went 23-4, won the Southern Conference, and finished ninth in the coaches' poll.

The team's thirteen wins in Big East play set a school record that remains. They won the program's first and only Big East tournament title. (WVU moved to the Big 12 in 2012.)

Senior forward Da'Sean Butler joined Jerry West and Rod Hundley as the only West Virginia players to score more than 2,000 points in their careers. He was named to two first-team All-America squads and won the Lowe's Senior CLASS Award.

Several other, less sweeping aspects of the season made it memorable. For instance, freshman center Deniz Kilicli sat out the first 21 games of the season. His terrible offense? He had played for a Turkish national team that had a professional player on it.

West Virginia beat Georgetown 60-58 for the Big East championship at Madison Square Garden in New York City. WVU's starting lineup that game — Butler, Wellington Smith, Kevin Jones, Devin Ebanks, and Truck Bryant — was all from the New

MOUNTAINEERS

York City metropolitan area.

In the second round of the NCAA Tournament versus Missouri, the Mountaineers had one 13-minute stretch in which they hit only one field goal. They still increased their lead by three points.

In the East Regional finals against top-seeded Kentucky, WVU incredibly did not make a two-point basket in the first half. The team was 0-for-16. The Mountaineers nevertheless won 73-66.

It was indeed a season Mountaineer fans will long remember.

Memory makes us who we are. Whether our memories appear as pleasant reverie or unnerving nightmares, they shape us and to a large extent determine both our actions and our reactions. Alzheimer's is so terrifying because it steals our memory from us, and in the process we lose ourselves. We disappear.

The greatest tragedy of our lives is that God remembers. In response to that photographic memory, he condemns us for our sin. Paradoxically, the greatest joy of our lives is that God remembers. In response to that memory, he came as Jesus to wash even the memory of our sins away.

For God, memory is a tool through which we encounter revival. At the Last Supper, Jesus instructed his disciples and us to remember. In sharing this unique meal with fellow believers and remembering Jesus and his actions, we meet Christ again, not just as a memory but as an actual living presence. To remember is to keep our faith alive.

A trophy carries dust. Memories last forever.

— *Mary Lou Retton*

**Because we remember Jesus,
God will not remember our sins.**

DAY 73

THINK ABOUT IT

Read Job 28.

"The fear of the Lord — that is wisdom, and to shun evil is understanding" (v. 28).

For Geno Smith, football has always been more of a mental game than a physical one.

From 2009-2012, Smith established himself as the greatest passing quarterback in WVU football history. He rewrote the school record book, finishing with the career records for total offense, passing yards, pass completions, pass attempts, passing efficiency, touchdown passes, and completion percentage.

The logical conclusion for all that success would be that Smith was the most talented athlete on the field. Not so, he would counter. For Smith, the difference was mental. Truth be told, while he was in Morgantown, Smith was a football nerd.

"I honestly don't think I'm that great of a player," he once said. "But I understand the game and I'm far ahead of my peers when it comes to that."

Head coach Dana Holgorsen backed up Smith's assessment that his mental acuity and not his physical ability was the primary reason for his gridiron success. "He's a very intelligent kid," the head Mountaineer once said. "His goal in life, his focus in life, is to learn as much about football as he possibly can. He loves to read. He loves to draw. But I guarantee you, when he's reading and drawing, he's still thinking about football."

MOUNTAINEERS

Smith was so focused on football in high school that despite being a naturally gifted artist, he turned down admission to a fine arts magnet school to concentrate on football.

Following his record-setting performance in the 70-63 shootout win over Baylor his senior season, Smith celebrated in his own unique way. He returned to the football building to study videos of the next opponent. He was just being Geno Smith, the thinking man's football player.

You're also a thinking person. Logic and reason are part of your psyche. A coach's bad call frustrates you, and your children's inexplicable behavior flummoxes you. Our leaders' failure to come up with reasonable solutions to our nation's problems leaves you talking to yourself. Why can't people just think things through?

That goes for matters of faith too. Jesus doesn't tell you to turn your brain off when you walk into a church or open the Bible. In fact, when you seek Jesus, you seek him heart, soul, body, and mind. The mind of the master should be the master of your mind so that you consider every situation in your life through the critical lens of the mind of Christ. With your head and your heart, you encounter God, who is, after all, the true source of wisdom.

To know Jesus is not to stop thinking; it is to start thinking divinely.

90 percent of the game is mental, [so I can] end up with those crazy numbers [in a game] because I'm always making the right decision.
— *Geno Smith on why he is successful on the field*

Since God is the source of all wisdom,
it's only logical that you encounter him
with your mind as well as your emotions.

TOP SECRET

Read Romans 2:1-16.

"This will take place on the day when God will judge
men's secrets through Jesus Christ, as my gospel declares"
(v. 16).

Jim Carlen had a secret, and he won a bowl game with it.

In four seasons as WVU's head football coach from 1966-69, Carlen went 25-13-3. He is credited by some with moving the Mountaineer program into the big time when he convinced the school's leaders to leave the Southern Conference and compete as an independent. He worked to modernize the program's facilities, going so far as to lobby for road improvements to connect the Morgantown campus to the southern parts of the state.

His best team was his last one, the 1969 squad that went 9-1, losing only to fifth-ranked Penn State. The team earned a berth in the Peach Bowl against South Carolina.

WVU's offense was in trouble. Star receiver Oscar Patrick was out with a knee injury; the team's second-best receiver had cut class before the bowl game and Carlen had benched him. Thus, passing was a problem and the Gamecocks knew it. Carlen had to do something, so he prepared a great big secret.

His offense ran the veer that season. The team used a split-back formation with quick handoffs that required backs Bob Gresham, Jim Braxton, and Eddie Williams to read the linemen's blocks and react to where the hole was.

MOUNTAINEERS

Before the bowl, Carlen and assistant Jim Flick went down to the University of Texas and studied the wishbone. They shocked Carolina when they lined up with no wide receiver and Williams as a true fullback. From the wishbone, they ran veer plays.

Carolina's defense spent the game waiting to react to the halfback dive. Instead, the Mountaineers kept giving the ball to the fullback inside. "They never even touched him," Carlen said.

Williams ran 35 times for 208 yards; WVU won 14-3.

As Jim Carlen was about his new offense for the bowl game, we have to be vigilant about the personal information we prefer to keep secret. Much information about us — from credit reports to what movies we stream and what clothes we buy — is available to anyone persistent enough to get it. In our information age, people we don't know may know a lot about us, and some of them may use this information to do us harm.

While diligence may allow us to be reasonably successful in keeping some secrets from the world at large, we should never deceive ourselves into believing we are keeping secrets from God. God knows everything about us, including the things we wouldn't want proclaimed at church. All our sins, shortcomings, mistakes, failures, quirks, prejudices, and desires — God knows all our would-be secrets.

But here's something God hasn't kept a secret: No matter what he knows about us, he loves us still.

South Carolina had never seen us do that.
— Jim Carlen on his secret offense

We have no secrets before God, and it's no secret that he nevertheless loves us still.

DYNASTY

Read 2 Samuel 7:8-17.

"Your house and your kingdom will endure forever before me; your throne will be established forever" (v. 16).

In relative anonymity, one WVU athletic program has built an NCAA dynasty: the rifle team.

The NCAA established the shooting championships in 1980. The Mountaineers were the runners-up the first three seasons before winning their first title. The dynasty had begun.

In 1998, the Mountaineers won their twelfth national championship. At one point during that stretch, they won six straight crowns. They were the runners-up three other times.

After a dry spell set in, Jon Hammond was summoned in 2006 to re-establish the dynasty. He has done so. In the 2016-17 season, the Mountaineers won their fifth straight national title and their eighth straight conference championship. The national crown was the program's nineteenth. Thus, through the 2016-17 season, WVU had won half of the NCAA titles.

Hammond's first two teams went 14-7 during the season as he set about fulfilling the promise he had made to rebuild the WVU dynasty. Since then, the record across the regular seasons has been an incredible 100-7 with four undefeated campaigns.

Five shooters from the 2016-17 squad were named All-America. Sophomore Ginny Thraser (See Devotion No. 20.) was the national Rifle Athlete of the Year. Milica Babic won the national Freshman of the Year prize. Senior Jean-Pierre Lucas, junior Elizabeth Gratz, and freshman Morgan Phillips were First-Team All-Americas.

Hammond knows of the extra pressure shooting for WVU now carries. "The expectations from media, fans, [and] parents are not something we can control," he said after his team won the 2015-16 title. What the team can control is keeping the dynasty alive.

Inevitably, someone will snap the string of WVU rifle championships. History teaches us that kingdoms, empires, countries, and even sports programs rise and fall. Dynasties end as events and circumstances conspire and align to snap all winning streaks.

Your life is like that; you win some and lose some. You get a promotion on Monday and your son gets arrested on Friday. You breeze through your annual physical but your dog dies. You finally line up a date with that cutie next door and get sent out of town on business.

Only one dynasty will never end because it is based upon an everlasting promise from God. God promised David the king an enduring line in the appearance of one who would establish God's kingdom forever. That one is Jesus Christ, the reigning king of God's eternal and unending dynasty.

The only way to lose out on that one is to stand on the sidelines and not get in the game.

I came [to WVU] because this was the best place to give me a chance to win a national title.
— Garrett Spurgeon, class of '16, who shot for four national champions

**All dynasties and win streaks end except the one
God established with Jesus as its king; this one
never loses and never will.**

GOD'S HOUSE

Read 2 Samuel 7:1-7.

"I have not dwelt in a house from the day I brought the Israelites up out of Egypt to this day. I have been moving from place to place with a tent as my dwelling" (v. 6).

Critics ridiculed it as "Bucky's Castle." Now, decades after its construction, "the WVU Coliseum still stands as one of the nation's supreme showrooms for college basketball."

Bucky Waters coached the WVU men's basketball team from 1965-69. His record was 70-41; his 1967 squad won the Southern Conference, landing the team in the NCAA Tournament.

The idea for a new basketball facility to replace the Field House first began to circulate in 1958. Each year, athletic director Red Brown included in his annual report a few paragraphs expressing the need for a new facility. His request was largely ignored.

By the mid-1960s, though, the university was undergoing its biggest expansion ever. The student population had doubled in ten years. That meant new buildings for all those new students.

In 1967, the state legislature expressed its willingness to consider a bond for the construction of a new basketball arena, a new law school, and an addition to the Medical Center. What followed, not surprisingly, was an old-fashioned turf war.

The dean of the law school derided the basketball arena as "Bucky's Castle." "Why do we need this thing?" he asked. "We need a law school and we need classrooms." Waters conceded it was a good argument.

But Brown had a stroke of genius when he turned away from the idea of a stand-alone basketball facility by getting the School of Physical Education involved. That worked. On Sept. 23, 1967, the board met and gave Waters an audience. He had ten minutes. "That's ten minutes for $10 million," the coach said.

The funding was a go. Work crews were on site the following week. The project was completed before the 1970-71 school year.

Buildings such as the WVU Coliseum often play pivotal roles in our lives, and we sometimes become sentimentally attached to them. A favorite restaurant. A football stadium or basketball gymnasium. The house you grew up in.

But what about a church? How important is that particular facility to you? Is it just the place where you were married? Where you were baptized? Is it nothing more than a house of memories or where you go to out of habit to placate the spouse?

Or is it the place where you regularly go to meet God? After all, that's what a church building really is: a place built expressly for God. It's God house. Long ago, the only place God could visit his people was in a lousy tent. Nowadays, churches serve as the site where God's people meet both to worship and to encounter him.

In a church alive with a true love of God, he is always there. Whether you find him or not depends on how hard you look. And whether you're searching for him with your heart.

You can kiss the Mountaineer basketball tradition good-bye.
— Bucky Waters on the result of not building a new basketball facility

**When you visit God in his house,
do you find him there?**

DAY 77

HOPE CHEST

Read Psalm 42.

"Put your hope in God, for I will yet praise him, my Savior and my God" (v. 5b).

There were 11 minutes remaining on the clock, but there may as well have been zero. No amount of time could save West Virginia." In other words, the Mountaineers' situation was hopeless.

On Oct. 15, 2005, WVU hosted Louisville in the biggest game of the season. The winner would gain the inside path to the Big East title and a BCS bowl berth. And WVU didn't show up.

Louisville led 17-0 at halftime, and a bleak situation turned hopeless with 11:42 to play and West Virginia trailing 24-7. That's when starting quarterback Adam Bednarik went down with a foot injury. Into the game came Pat White, "a gangly freshman about whom much was whispered but little was known."

WVU was finished, done. Fans were leaving so fast the place looked like a fire drill. But White and freshman running back Steve Slaton etched their names in WVU lore by leading what is perhaps the most famous comeback in school football history.

The unintentional change in quarterbacks brought the moribund WVU offense to life. Slaton scored on a 3-yard run to make it 24-14 with eight minutes left. After Pat McAfee pulled off his first-ever onside kick, he kicked a field goal with 4:35 left. 24-17.

Then with exactly one minute left, Slaton capped off a 40-yard drive with a 1-yard touchdown run. The game went into the first of three overtime sessions.

In the third OT, Slaton scored his fifth touchdown of the game, and the Mountaineers notched the two-point conversion. Louisville answered with a score. On the conversion, West Virginia blitzed and safety Eric Wicks tackled the Cardinal quarterback.

Once out of hope and almost out of time, WVU had won 46-44.

Only when a life has no hope does it become not worth the living. To hope is not merely to want something; that is desire or wishful thinking. To produce hope, desire must be coupled with some degree of expectation.

Therein lies the great problem. We may wish for a lot of money, relief from our diabetes, world peace, or a diet plan that lets us lose weight while we stuff ourselves with doughnuts, cheeseburgers, and fried chicken. Our hopes, however, must be firmly grounded, or they will inevitably lead us to disappointment, shame, and disaster. In other words, false hopes ruin us.

One of the most basic issues of our lives, therefore, becomes discovering or locating that in which we can place our hope. Where can we find sure promises for a future that we can count on? Where can we place our hope with realistic expectations that we can live securely even though some of the promises we rely on are yet to be delivered?

In God. In God and God alone lies our hope.

A play that was supposed to kill any hopes of a comeback sparked an era of unprecedented success for an unsuspecting program.
— Writer Craig Meyer on the injury to Adam Bednarik vs. Louisville

**God and his sustaining power are the source of
the only meaningful hope possible in our lives.**

DAY 78

CLOTHES HORSE

Read Genesis 37:1-11.

"Israel loved Joseph more than all his children, because he was the son of his old age: and he made him a coat of many colours" (v. 3 KJV).

Sam Huff got a suit of clothes as he had been promised, all right. Those "new" duds just weren't exactly what he expected.

Huff is a Mountaineer legend. He was a four-year letterwinner (1952-55) and three-year starter at guard and tackle. He was an All-American as a senior who also earned first-team Academic All-American honors. In 1982, he became the second WVU player to be inducted into both the college and pro football halls of fame. (Joe Stydahar was the first.) His number 75 was retired in 2005.

Huff played for Art Lewis, who from 1950-59 became WVU's winningest coach to that time with 58 wins. Lewis' toughness was legendary. As an undergrad at Ohio University, he fell so hard during a game that "his left arm popped out at the elbow, with the bone protruding." He kept on playing until finally he began to feel ill. He called timeout and then calmly walked into the locker room.

Lewis' method of determining playing time was simple: He used "man-on-man, one-on-one, physical confrontations" at practice. As Huff put it, the toughest guy started. But Lewis also took up for his players, and they loved him for it.

When Huff was a junior facing Penn State's great tackle Rosey

Grier, Lewis told Huff he would buy him a new suit if he could handle Grier. Huff played so well in WVU's 19-14 upset that the coach, "mortified that he was actually going to have to buy an expensive oversized suit . . ., hemmed and hawed, trying to find a way out of his predicament while still trying to keep his word."

Lewis solved his problem by pulling one of his old suits out of the closet. He had his wife "wrap it in a box like it was brand new, and he gave it to Huff in front of the team."

Contemporary society proclaims that it's all about the clothes. Buy that new suit — like the one Sam Huff didn't get — or dress, those new shoes, and all the accessories, and you'll be a new person. The changes are only cosmetic, though; under those clothes, you're the same person. Consider Joseph, for instance, prancing about in his pretty new clothes; he was still a spoiled little tattle-tale whom his brothers detested enough to sell into slavery.

Jesus never taught that we should run around half-naked or wear only second-hand clothes from the local mission. He did warn us, though, against making consumer items such as clothes a priority in our lives. A follower of Christ seeks to emulate Jesus not through material, superficial means such as wearing special clothing like a robe and sandals. Rather, the disciple desires to match Jesus' inner beauty and serenity — whether the clothes the Christian wears are the sables of a king or the rags of a pauper.

You can't call [golf] a sport. You don't run, jump, you don't shoot, you don't pass. All you have to do is buy some clothes that don't match.
— Former all-star second baseman Steve Sax

Where Jesus is concerned, clothes don't make the person; faith does.

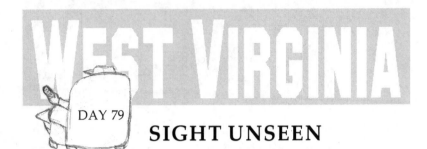

SIGHT UNSEEN

Read 2 Corinthians 5:6-10.

"We live by faith, not by sight" (v. 7).

Shelton Gibson's catch turned the game West Virginia's way even though he couldn't really see the ball because a defender was ripping his helmet off.

On Oct. 1, 2016, the 3-0 Mountaineers were in real danger of losing their Big-12 opener at home against Kansas State. They trailed 16-3 late in the third quarter. Head coach Dana Holgorsen kept asking his players on the sideline who was going to step up. One player he called by name was Gibson, a junior receiver. "I had to make a play," Gibson said. He did.

With 1:39 to go in the third, quarterback Skyler Howard let fly with a bomb Gibson's way. "I trust him to go up and get the ball no matter what the situation," Howard said.

Usually, though, when Gibson went up to get a ball, he could see it. Not necessarily this time. He had leaped and was stretching in the air when a State defender wrapped his hands around Gibson's helmet. What happened next was unintentional: Gibson's helmet started coming off. By the time the ball was only inches away, he "was almost blind to the play."

"I could only see the ball through the holes in my chin strap," he said, "because it was over my eyes when my helmet was coming off. I could also see a little out of the top of my face mask."

Despite not being able to really see the ball, Gibson made the

MOUNTAINEERS

catch for a 52-yard completion. His grab set up a 1-yard touchdown run with 13:41 left to play. At 16-10, WVU was back in the game and the momentum had turned.

Later, the Mountaineers went 57 yards in nine plays for what would be the game-winning score. Scrambling to escape pressure, Howard found Jovon Durante for a 7-yard touchdown with 6:11 to play. Mike Molina's extra point gave West Virginia a 17-16 lead.

When K-State missed a field goal with 2:03 left, WVU ran out the clock. The 17-16 final was on the scoreboard for all to see.

To close our eyes or to be engulfed suddenly by total darkness plunges us into a world in which we struggle to function. Our world and our place in it are built on our eyesight, so much so that we tout "Seeing is believing." If we can't see it, we don't believe it. Perhaps the most famous proponent of this attitude was the disciple Thomas, who refused to believe Jesus had risen from the dead until he saw the proof for himself.

But our sight carries us only so far because its usefulness is restricted to the physical world. Eyesight has no place in spiritual matters. We don't "see" God; we don't "see" Jesus; we don't "see" God at work in the physical world. And yet we know God; we know Jesus; we know God is in control. We "know" all that because as the children of God, we live by faith and not by sight.

Looking through the eyes of faith, we come to understand that believing is seeing.

I was watching the replay [of the catch]. I've probably seen it 20 times.
— Shelton Gibson on why he was late for post-game interviews

In God's physical world, seeing is believing;
in God's spiritual world, believing is seeing.

DAY 80

AD MAN

Read Mark 1:21-28.

"News about him spread quickly over the whole region"
(v. 28).

Some wags claimed that WVU publicist Eddie Barrett had the easiest job in the country when it came to Mountaineer basketball. That really wasn't the case, however, as he faced some real problems in his efforts to publicize the school's players.

Barrett was West Virginia's athletics publicity director from 1951-67. He brought WVU into the modern age of sports information. In 2010, he was inducted into the WVU Sports Hall of Fame.

Why would anyone consider his job so easy? It was said he "just waited to see who arrived on campus during the fall semester to begin promoting another basketball All-American." Since he worked during the golden age of Mountaineer basketball, there may be an element of truth in that.

First, there was All-American center Mark Workman in 1952. Then came Hot Rod Hundley (1956 and 1957), Jerry West (1959 and 1960), and Rod Thorn (1962 and 1963). Center Lloyd Sharrar was a second-team All-America in 1958, and guard Lee Patrone (who once dove into the Ohio River to save a drowning woman) was a Helms Foundation third teamer in 1961. Barrett also publicized All-American footballers Sam Huff and Bruce Bosley.

But it wasn't necessarily easy. In a time when the media didn't devote much time or space to college basketball, West Virginia

MOUNTAINEERS

was at a decided disadvantage. The biggest problem was that the Mountaineers played in the second-tier Southern Conference. The school also didn't have a legacy of basketball greatness. Despite some dogged persistence, Barrett could not persuade *Sports Illustrated*'s college basketball writer to do a feature on West.

Probably the biggest coup of Barrett's tenure came when NBC agreed to televise the Holy Cross game on Feb. 7, 1959. The game was the first televised event carried live and direct from WVU.

Commercials and advertisements for products, goods, and services inundate us. Watch NASCAR: Decals cover the cars and the drivers' uniforms. Turn on your computer: Ads pop up. TV, radio, newspapers, billboards, every square inch of every wall — everyone's one trying to get the word out the best way possible.

Jesus was no different in that he used the most effective and efficient means of advertising he had at his disposal to spread his message of salvation and hope among the masses. That was word of mouth.

In his ministry, Jesus didn't isolate himself; instead, he moved from town to town among the common folks, preaching, teaching, and healing. Those who encountered Jesus then told others about their experience, thus spreading the news about the good news. Almost two millennia later, nothing's really changed. Speaking to someone else about Jesus remains the best way to get the word out, and the best advertisement of all is a changed life.

Jerry [West] was kept under wraps. He [was] taken out of games early.
— A frustrated Eddie Barrett on trying to publicize Jerry West

The best advertising for Jesus is word of mouth,
telling others what he has done for you.

DAY 81

TRAGEDY

Read Job 1; 2:1-10.

"In all this, Job did not sin by charging God with wrongdoing" (v. 1:22).

The Mountaineers once suffered the tragedy of having a player die from injuries suffered during a game.

The 1-1-1 Mountaineers played Bethany on Nov. 12, 1910. Captain and halfback Rudolph Munk was the star of the team. A versatile athlete who had played quarterback the season before, he was also the shortstop on the baseball team. His touchdown and field goal gave West Virginia an early 9-0 lead. With WVU threatening to score again late in the game, Munk was the lead blocker on a running play. What happened remains a matter of dispute and conjecture to this day.

Bethany's right end, whose name survives only as McCoy, delivered a blow to the base of Munk's neck that left him prostrate on the field. Thrown out of the game, McCoy reportedly left without protest or excuse or even looking down at the injured player. Testimony was inconclusive as to whether the blow was a deliberate attempt to injure Munk and get him out of the game.

Subsequent investigations revealed McCoy was a ringer who may have been brought in to help avenge a scoreless tie earlier in the season. He had withdrawn from Bethany three weeks earlier.

Munk was rushed to a hospital but died without regaining consciousness. He died that night from brain swelling and a blood clot at the base of the cerebellum.

Indignation and anger naturally ran high in the wake of the tragedy. Coroner W.W. Rogers initially issued a warrant charging McCoy with murder. Two days after the game, the coroner's jury ruled Munk's death was an accident. The warrant was withdrawn.

The university council cancelled the remainder of the season.

While we may receive them in varying degrees, suffering and tragedy are par for life's course. What we do with tragedy when it inevitably strikes us determines to a great extent how we live the rest of our lives.

We can — in accordance with the bitter suggestion that Job's wife offered — "Curse God and die," or we can trust God and live. That is, we can plunge into endless despair or we can lean upon the power of a transcendent faith in an almighty God who offers us hope in our darkest hours.

We don't have to understand tragedy such as the senseless death of Rudolph Munk. We don't have to like it or believe there's anything fair about it. What we must do in such times, however, is trust in God's all-powerful love for us and his promise that all things will work for good for those who love him.

In choosing a life of ongoing trust in God in the face of our suffering, we prevent the greatest tragedy of all: that of a soul being cast into Hell.

There is a great demand for this game among the [athletes] but how about the parents whose hearts are broken from the result of the game?
— Morgantown New Dominion *on the death of Rudolph Munk*

Tragedy can drive us into despair and death or into the life-sustaining arms of almighty God.

DAY 82

ZINGERS

Read Luke 20:9-19.

"The teachers of the law and the chief priests looked for a way to arrest him . . . because they knew he had spoken . . . against them" (v. 19).

The opposing head coach insulted Don Nehlen at a press conference. The result was a riled up Mountaineer team that pulled off one of the biggest upsets in the school's bowl history.

Nehlen's second team went 8-3 in 1981 and landed in the Peach Bowl. The Florida Gators were the loyal opposition, and nobody but nobody gave the Mountaineers a chance. The Las Vegas oddsmakers declared the Gators to be the lock of the bowl season.

Nehlen wasn't convinced. "I thought we had a real chance," he said, "because that 1981 team got better all the time." What the Mountaineers needed was to play the game with an attitude; they needed a chip on their collective shoulders. The Gator head man unintentionally gave them one.

Nehlen and his captains, tight end Mark Raugh and quarterback Oliver Luck, attended a press conference two days before the game. When the Florida coach spoke, he revealed he had no idea what Nehlen's name was. He kept calling him "Nellen." "It was no big deal to me," Nehlen said.

But it was to Raugh. When he left the press conference, he "was so mad he was spitting his words," which included some less than flattering names for the Gator coach. As soon as he rejoined

MOUNTAINEERS

his teammates, Raugh made sure they knew about the insult.

The defensive coaches came up with a blitzing scheme to confuse the Gator quarterback. The offensive coaches scripted most of the first-quarter plays and stuck with it. They also drew up a screen pass to running back Mickey Walczak that Florida never adjusted to.

It all worked for a resounding 26-6 blasting of the Gators.

There's nothing like a good insult to rile us up as Florida's coach did to the Mountaineers. We take an insult — even an unintentional one — exactly as it is meant: personally.

Few people throughout history can match Jesus, of all people, for delivering a well-placed zinger, and few insults throughout history can match the one he tossed at the religious authorities in Luke 20. Jesus' remarks were so accurate and so severe that the targets of his insult responded by seeking to have him arrested.

Using a vineyard as the centerpiece of an extensive allegory, Jesus insulted the priests and their lackeys by declaring that they had insulted God in rejecting his rule over them. They had sought to own God's kingdom for themselves.

They were truly just a bunch of hypocrites. But before we get too smug, we need to take a good look around. Little has changed. We still seek to live our lives on our terms, not God's. The world is in such a mess because we want to run God's vineyard, instead of surrendering to him. Jesus delivered that insult right at us.

Coach, I'm telling you [he] will know your name after the game is over.
— An angry Mark Raugh to Don Nehlen after the press conference

In insulting the priests for rebelling against God,
Jesus delivered a zinger right at us.

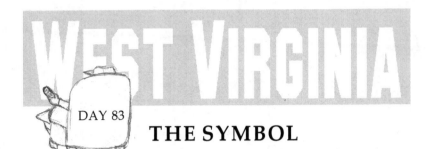

DAY 83

THE SYMBOL

Read Mark 15:16-32.

"Let this Christ, this king of Israel, come down now from the cross, that we may see and believe" (v. 32a).

The best-known image and symbol of the university and the state wears buckskin, carries a rifle disguised as a musket, and wears a cap with eyes. It's WVU's Mountaineer.

Graduate student Troy Clemons donned the buckskin and the coonskin cap for the 2016-17 and 2017-18 school years. He followed Michael Garcia, who also toted the musket for two terms and said being the mascot was "the coolest thing I'll ever do in my life."

The job keeps getting bigger, and it was already demanding. In 2012, for instance, mascot Jonathan Kimble traveled about 2,500 miles in one week making personal appearances.

The first Mountaineer mascot was in 1927, but for some reason he wasn't officially recognized by the university. The first "official" mascot was Boyd H. "Slim" Arnold in 1937. In 1990, Natalie Tennant, who was elected West Virginia's Secretary of State in 2008, was the first female Mountaineer. (Rebecca Durst in 2009 is the other.) Tennant recalled that not everyone was happy about her selection. People threw cups at her and taunted her.

When William "Buck" Rogers was the Mountaineer in 1963, today's rigorous application process wasn't in place. He simply saw an ad in the student newspaper, applied, and got the job. In the Navy game that season, the Midshipmen ran out of powder for their cannon. Rogers loaned them some, and as a reward, their fans passed him up and down the stands.

Writer Laura Wilcox Rote said, "The Mountaineer carries not just the weight of his mascot's uniform, but the weight of West Virginia on his back." Thus, in the atmosphere of today's big-time college sports, the Mountaineer's outfit may have remained the same over the years, but the demands and pressure on the student mascot have increased. It is a job to be treated seriously.

Symbols are powerful factors in our lives. Witness, for instance, the power the Mountaineer has to invigorate a sense of pride in both West Virginia the state and West Virginia the university.

Some symbols — such as company logos like the swoosh and the golden arches — are carefully chosen. Others seem to arrive as if by accident or through custom. Christianity's most recognized and beloved symbol is one of the latter. It is the cross, perhaps the most unlikely choice for a symbol in history.

After all, in its time, the cross was a symbol for the ultimate ignominy, the means of execution for the Roman Empire's most scorned criminals and lowlifes. And our lord died on one of them.

Yet, today, for Christians to boldly proclaim their faith for everyone to see, they need only wear a cross. What once symbolized death and despair has become a symbol of hope and love. Such is the transforming power of God through Jesus.

I will strive every day to serve our state and our University in a way that makes all Mountaineers proud.
> — *Senior Trevor Kiess, 2018-19 Mountaineer Mascot*

As it did with the cross, God's love can take our ugly lives and make them beautiful.

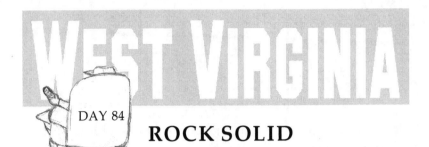

ROCK SOLID

Read Luke 6:46-49.

"I will show you what he is like who comes to me and hears my words and puts them into practice. He is like a man building a house, who dug down deep and laid the foundation on rock" (vv. 47-48).

To mold her sport into the national power it is today, Nikki Izzo-Brown first had to lay a foundation. It wasn't easy.

Through the 2018 season, Izzo-Brown was the only head coach West Virginia's women's soccer has ever had. The Mountaineers' resume includes eleven conference crowns, six league tournament titles, and nineteen straight trips to the NCAA Tournament. 2016's 23-2-2 squad is the only team in Big 12 history to shut out all of its league opponents and was the NCAA runner-up.

Izzo-Brown's first question when she arrived on campus in 1995 was, "OK. Where's my office?" She didn't have one. WVU "knew they needed to start a program because of Title IX, but I don't think they'd really looked into it," she said.

She spent her first few months in a former first-aid office, sharing space with tennis coach Ed Dixon. Her players shared Mountaineer Field with the football team. Head coach Don Nehlen once told Izzo-Brown her girls were a distraction to his football players. She spoke once to a PE class, and a football player asked her, "Coach, what do you do at the end of the games when the girls are crying and you have to hug them?"

MOUNTAINEERS

Opposing coaches thought Izzo-Brown's program was a joke at first. After all, her first players were all freshmen and sophomores, some of whom just weren't good enough. She had to fight for assistant coaches, locker rooms, and field space.

It didn't matter. Instead of worrying about everything, Izzo-Brown took the approach that if her players and she outworked everyone else, they would earn the respect they deserved.

So she steadfastly went about laying the foundation for success.

Like WVU's entire athletics program, your life is an ongoing project, a work in progress. As with any complex construction job, if your life is to be stable, it must have a solid foundation, which holds everything up and keeps everything together.

R. Alan Culpepper said in *The New Interpreter's Bible*, "We do not choose whether we will face severe storms in life; we only get to choose the foundation on which we will stand." In other words, tough times are inevitable. If your foundation isn't rock-solid, you will have nothing on which to stand as those storms buffet you, nothing to keep your life from flying apart into a cycle of disappointment and destruction.

But when the foundation is solid and sure, you can take the blows, stand strong, recover, and live with joy and hope. Only one foundation is sure and foolproof: Jesus Christ. Everything else you build upon will fail you.

Jesus Christ is the rock upon which I stand.
— Heisman Trophy winner Danny Wuerffel

In the building of your life, you must start with a foundation in Jesus Christ, or the first trouble that shows up will knock you down.

IN THE BAD TIMIES

Read Philippians 1:3-14.

"What has happened to me has really served to advance the gospel. . . . Because of my chains, most of the brothers in the Lord have been encouraged to speak the word of God more courageously and fearlessly" (vv. 12, 14).

Football provided Noel Devine with an escape from the maelstrom that was his life as a child.

As a Mountaineer running back from 2007-10, Devine rushed for 4,315 yards, a total that places him third all-time in career rushing yards behind Avon Cobourne and Pat White.

Devine's maternal grandmother introduced him to football when he was 12. It wasn't to continue his happy, carefree childhood days. In truth, he had "been bearing adult-sized burdens as long as he could remember." Football was a way to take the child's mind off his grief.

Three months after Noel's birth in 1988, his father died from AIDS. He was 32. Thus, "the months following his birth weren't filled with joy but panic" as his grandmother repeatedly and frantically had her infant grandson tested for AIDS.

From the time Devine could remember, his mother was dying of the same disease as she also battled a cocaine addiction. Devine recalled that when he was 8 or 9, he raided her purse and flushed the cocaine he found there down the toilet to keep her from smoking it. She died in 2000; she was 31; her orphaned son was 11.

Devine's grandmother years before had been appointed his legal guardian, but she failed to provide him with a stable home. In 1997, she was arrested for drug trafficking and was jailed for 29 months. "It took a long time for me to forgive myself," she said.

She did, however, in the summer of 2000 after Devine's mom had died in January, sign him up for Pop Warner football. From the first day of practice, he was a star. The boy who had stopped being a boy long ago had found some good times in his life.

We all experience hard, tragic times, though perhaps not to the extent the young Noel Devine did. Loved ones die. Your company downsizes and you lose your job. Your biopsy looks suspicious.

Bad times happen regardless of your faith. Christianity is not the equivalent of a Get-out-of-Jail-Free card, granting us a lifelong exemption from either the least or the worst pain the world has to offer. While Jesus promises us he will be there to lead us through the valleys, he never promises that we will not enter them.

The question therefore becomes how you handle the bad times. You can buckle to your knees in despair, cry "Why me?" and rail against God for the unfairness of it all. Or you can hit your knees in prayer and ask God, "What do I do with this?"

Setbacks and tragedies are opportunities to reveal and to develop true character and abiding faith. Your faithfulness — not your skipping merrily along through life without pain — is what reveals the depth of your love for God.

Life is too short to dwell on the past. God forgives; forgive and forget.
— Noel Devine on the bad times of his childhood

Faithfulness to God requires faith
even in — especially in — the bad times.

DAY 86

NO JOKE!

Read Romans 12:9-21.

"Do not be overcome by evil, but overcome evil with good" (v. 21).

The Mountaineers once played in a bowl game so slung together that the whole affair wound up being little more than a joke.

Junior receiver Bob Dunlevy caught 18 passes for 279 yards and a pair of touchdowns in 1964, but his biggest reception was his 50-yard grab for the game-winning touchdown in the 28-27 upset of Syracuse. After the game, the Liberty Bowl invited West Virginia to play Utah in its first-ever indoor game.

The Liberty Bowl's first five games had been played before sparse crowds in Philadelphia in such awful weather that writers had derisively tagged the contest with such labels as the "Deep Freeze Bowl" and the "You're-Out-of-Your-Mind Bowl." When Atlantic City offered the convention center, bowl officials jumped.

Perhaps they shouldn't have. In this time before Astroturf and the like, a four-inch thick grass surface with two-inch padding was hauled in and placed over the concrete flooring. Artificial lighting was used to help keep the grass alive.

The end zones were eight yards deep instead of ten. The teams' dressing rooms were on a stage above the end zone. "There was no place to even hang your clothes," Dunlevy recalled. The folks from the Miss America Pageant were not too happy with having to share their stage with flying footballs.

MOUNTAINEERS

Writers covered the game for the TV gimmick it was. One wrote that spectators could watch the grass grow if the game was dull. Another installed the grass as a three-point favorite in the game.

The game was a joke, too, as Utah won easily, leading the convention center's public address announcer to famously declare, "Only two minutes left in the game. . . . Thank God!"

Certainly the Bible is not a repository of side-splitting jokes, though some theologians have posited that Jesus' parables were actually sort of jokes for his time. Have you heard the one about the son who left his rich father and went to live with pigs?

No, the Gospel and its message of salvation and hope is serious stuff. Christians take it as such and well they should. Yet though many Christians might well vilify anyone who treats Jesus as a joke, those same persons themselves treat some aspects of Jesus' teachings as little more than gags not to be taken seriously.

Sexual purity, for instance. How outdated is that? And the idea of expecting answers to our prayers. What a silly notion! Surely Jesus was jesting when he spoke of tithing. How laughable is it to live performing selfless acts for others without getting the credit! And polls consistently reveal that about half of America's Christians don't believe in Hell. In other words, Jesus was joking.

No, he wasn't. If we think any of what Jesus taught us is a joke, then the joke's on us — and it's not very funny.

WVU chose to defend the boardwalk while Utah picked the Miss America pageant stage.
— Columnist Red Smith, making a joke of the '64 Liberty Bowl

Jesus wasn't joking; if we really love him, then we will live in the manner he prescribed for us.

DAY 87

FOOD FOR THOUGHT

Read Genesis 9:1-7.

"Everything that lives and moves will be food for you. Just as I gave you the green plants, I now give you everything"
(v. 3).

Food may have played a part in Zach Abraham's landing a football scholarship.

Coming out of high school in 1991, Abraham passed on several offers from small colleges to walk on as a wide receiver at WVU. He knew that he would have to be something special to push a player with a scholarship to the bench. "I just got that mindset that I'm going to outwork [the scholarshipped players]," he said.

Abraham didn't play at all in 1991 and got into only one game in 1992. But he kept working and the coaches noticed, so much so that head Mountaineer Don Nehlen may well have believed Abraham to be one of his players on scholarship. An encounter centering on food corrected that notion.

One day as Nehlen left his office and headed for the training table where the staff and the athletes who were on scholarship ate their meals, he passed Abraham walking in the opposite direction to round up his own dinner. "Hey, Zach," the coach called. "Where are you going? Aren't you going to get something to eat?" "Coach," Abraham replied, "I don't have a scholarship, and I can't eat at the training table."

Nehlen was obviously puzzled. He then led Abraham to his

office and proceeded to load him up with bushel baskets full of vegetables. "We have a fan who insists on giving me some of his good vegetables, and he brings me so much that I don't know what to do with it. I give it away," Nehlen explained to his slightly befuddled player.

Shortly after that, Abraham was put on scholarship. As a senior in 1994, he started every game, catching 41 passes with six TDs.

Belly up to the buffet, boys and girls, for barbecue, sirloin steak, grilled chicken, and fried catfish with hush puppies. Rachael Ray's a household name; hamburger joints, pizza parlors, and taco stands lurk on every corner; and we have a TV channel devoted exclusively to food. We love our chow.

Food is one of God's really good ideas, but consider the complex divine plan that begins with a kernel and winds up with corn-on-the-cob slathered with butter and littered with salt. The creator of all life devised a downright fascinating and effective system in which living things are sustained and nourished physically through the sacrifice of other living things in a way similar to what Christ underwent to save us spiritually.

Whether it's fast food or home-cooked, practically everything we eat is a gift from God secured through a divine plan in which some plants and/or animals have given up their lives. Pausing to give thanks before we dive in seems the least we can do.

I had to walk about a mile to my apartment with all those vegetables.
— Zach Abraham on his coach's bounty

God created a system that nourishes us
through the sacrifice of other living things;
that's worth a thank-you.

TROUBLED TIMES

Read Nahum 1:1-8.

"The Lord is good, a refuge in times of trouble. He cares for those who trust in him" (v. 8).

The Mountaineer basketball team once ran into so much trouble on a road trip that an opponent let a player stay in the game even after he had fouled out so the contest could go on.

Basketball began as a consistent varsity sport at WVU in 1915, and the Mountaineers quickly earned a reputation for fielding tough teams. Thus, the 6-2 start in 1922 was no surprise, and the team was confident when it set out on a five-game road trip. They had no idea of the trouble that lay in store.

Misfortune struck early when forward Homer "Moose" Martin was felled by the flu. Martin was an early star, scoring 20 or more points in a game nine times and averaging 13.2 points per game for his 56-game career from 1919-22. He was eventually transported back to Morgantown. He had company before long when the flu sent guard Russ Meredith, an All-American tackle on the football team, back home.

The team's troubles weren't over. Coach Francis Stadsvold, who coached the Mountaineers for fourteen seasons, was left scrambling to field a team when forward Pierre Hill and center Roy "Legs" Hawley, who would serve as WVU's athletic director, were stricken. Down to only five players for a game against Princeton, the desperate Stadsvold ordered student manager J.B. Davis to

MOUNTAINEERS

suit up when a Mountaineer player was injured and had to leave the game temporarily.

In the game against CCNY, the Beavers were gracious enough to allow Robert Hawkins to continue to play after he fouled out. It was either that or the game was over since WVU didn't have any more healthy players.

And, oh, yes. The Mountaineers lost all five games on the trip.

For every West Virginia team in every game, trouble is going to come at some point. Winning or losing a particular contest is largely determined by how a team handles the trouble that comes its way during the ebb and flow of the action.

Life is no different. For each of us, trouble is going to come. The decisive factor for us all is how we handle it. What do we do when we're in trouble?

Admittedly, some troubles are worse and are more devastating than others. From health problems to financial woes to family problems, trouble can change our lives and everything about it.

The most fearsome danger, though, lies not in what trouble can do to us physically, emotionally, or psychologically, but in its potential to affect us spiritually. Do we respond to it by turning to the profane or to the profound? Does trouble wreck our faith in God or strengthen our trust in him?

Like everything of this world, trouble is temporal; God's love and power, however, are not. In God, we have a sure and certain refuge during the troubled times of our lives.

It was a trip filled with misadventure.
— Writer John Antonik on the ill-fated 1922 road trip

Trouble will come and God will be there for us.

DAY 89

FACING THE MUSIC

Read Psalm 98.

"Sing to the Lord a new song, for he has done marvelous things" (v. 1).

The university once had a rebellion in one of its student organization that resulted in competing groups. Of all things, it was the marching band!

The WVU Marching Band was first formed in 1901 as an all-male ROTC band of eight members. The band marched at halftime of football games but spent most of its time providing march music for military revues and parades. Whenever and wherever it appeared, the band always marched in strict military style. This was necessary because the band's instruments and equipment were owned by the federal government, which restricted their use to military functions.

In 1925, eleven non-ROTC students were allowed to join. Their non-military status meant, however, that they were not entitled to the same monetary benefits as the ROTC band members. They didn't like it, so they rebelled and formed their own marching band. Walter Mestrezat, the marching band's founding director, gave the rebels permission to play at halftime.

The school president stepped in and required the students to form a legitimate student organization. They pledged a Greek fraternity and formed what is now the WVU chapter of Kappa Kappa Psi. Only years later did the two bands merge into one.

MOUNTAINEERS

The band's modern era began in the 1950's and '60's, a time that saw the creation and adoption of the school's fight songs, "Hail West Virginia" and "Fight Mountaineers." The first women students joined the 88-member band in 1972. Today, "The Pride of West Virginia" has more than 330 members.

"Arguably the single-most important event in the history of [the band's] first century" occurred in 1997 when the band received the Sutler Trophy. It honored the group as the nation's most outstanding collegiate marching band for that year.

Maybe you can't play a lick or carry a tune in the proverbial bucket. Or perhaps you do know your way around a guitar or a keyboard and can sing "Hail West Virginia" on karaoke night without closing the joint down.

Unless you're a professional musician, however, how well you play or sing really doesn't matter. What counts is that you have music in your heart and sometimes you have to turn it loose.

Worshipping God has always included music in some form. That same boisterous and musical enthusiasm you exhibit when the WVU Marching Band plays at Mountaineer games should be a part of the joy you have in your personal worship of God.

Take a moment to count the blessings in your life, all gifts from God. Then consider that God loves you, he always will, and he has arranged through Jesus for you to spend eternity with him. How can that song God put in your heart not burst forth?

Just like music, sports elevates us to new levels of achievement.
— Drummer Randy Castillo

You call it music; others may call it noise;
sent God's way, it's called praise.

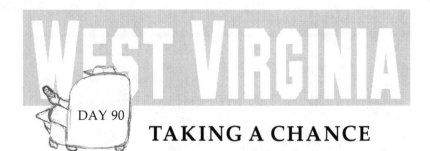

TAKING A CHANCE

Read Matthew 4:18-22.

"[A]nd immediately they left the boat and their father and followed him" (v. 22).

Pat McAfee took a chance that determined the course of his life. It involved lying, borrowing money, and playing poker.

McAfee completed his WVU punting and placekicker career as a senior in 2008 with a First-Team All-American season. He set the school record for career points scored with 384 and went on to a Pro Bowl career.

A national Punt, Pass & Kick champion, McAfee decided to concentrate on soccer, his first love, after Penn State reneged on a football scholarship offer. But his dad put together a tape of his son drilling field goals from as far away as 60 yards and sent it to every major college he could think of. Kent State was the only school that called. Kent State it was.

But McAfee was sitting in a senior physics class in December when his cell phone buzzed. It was a kicking guru inviting him to a national kicking competition in Miami. About a hundred college coaches would be there. Was he interested?

McAfee was, but he faced two big obstacles. First, his parents said he couldn't go; he had to honor his commitment to Kent State. Second, the trip would cost about $1,500, which he didn't have. Undeterred, he decided to take a wild chance. He lied to his parents, telling them he was sleeping over with a friend. Instead, he borrowed $100 from a friend and sneaked into a poker club in a local restaurant. Playing against grown men, he won $1,400.

McAfee used the money to buy a plane ticket. At the competition, he kicked nine straight field goals from 25 to 65 yards. Only at 70 yards did he miss; he was wide right. The day after he got home, WVU recruiting coordinator Tony Gibson met him in the school lunchroom and offered him a scholarship.

Our lives are the sum total of the chances we have taken — or have not taken — along the way. Every decision we make every day involves taking a chance. Maybe it will work out for the better; maybe it won't. We won't know unless we take a chance.

On the other hand, our regrets often center on the chances we pass by. The missed chance that has the most destructive and devastating effect on our lives comes when we fail to follow Jesus. He calls us all to surrender to him, to commit to him exactly as he called Simon, Andrew, James, and John.

What they did is unsettling. Without hesitation, without telling Jesus to give them time to think about it or wrap up the loose ends of their lives or tell all their friends good-bye, they walked away from a productive living and from their families. They took a chance on this itinerant preacher.

So must we. What have we got to lose? Nothing worthwhile. What have we got to gain? Everlasting life with God. If that's not worth taking a chance on, nothing is.

If I'd ended up at Kent State, who knows if I'd even have kicked?
— Pat McAfee, on how it might have been had he not taken a chance

To take a chance and surrender our lives to Jesus is to trade hopelessness and death for hope and life.

DAY 91

DETAIL ORIENTED

Read Matthew 25:31-46.

"The King will reply, ... 'I tell you the truth, whatever you did for one of the least of these brothers of mine, you did for me'" (v. 40).

Jim Carlen was so detail oriented that he sought to have the female fans stop wearing gloves to games and urged the administration to recruit more black female students.

Carlen arrived in Morgantown on Jan. 15, 1966, and immediately set about shaking things up. That meant he gave attention to every detail surrounding his football program.

For instance, he changed the team's uniforms and halted a longstanding tradition by ending the use of Jackson's Mill for a fall training camp. He said the campus facilities were better. He instituted an offseason conditioning program. Appreciating the value of promotion, he persuaded the school to produce some highlight shows and distribute them to television stations.

Carlen asked Associate Dean of Student Educational Services Betty Boyd if the girls could be talked into not wearing their hats and gloves to the games. Why in the world would he do such a thing? "My players can't hear the applause," he explained.

Keenly aware that WVU was losing too many of the state's best black players to out-of-state schools, he asked star receiver and cornerback John Mallory how the school could attract more black players. Mallory's answer was simple and surprising: Get some more black female students. Right away, Carlen began pressing the administration for a plan to recruit more minorities.

He issued stars to reward Mountaineer players for good play. His practices were timed right down to the minute. Eyeing the future, he held football clinics for kids. He encouraged Gov. Arch Moore, a WVU grad, to get moving on a highway plan. "I can't keep losing Bluefield boys to Virginia Tech," he told the governor.

As every detail of his job as head football coach was important to Jim Carlen, so should we tend carefully to the details of our faith life. Our confession of Jesus as our savior sometime in the past doesn't necessarily mean we are ready for his return now. Our faith must be alive and well today; we must live each day emulating our Lord in our service to him and to others.

The details of daily spiritual living — of which attending church is one part — ensure our faith is alive and vibrant. God expects us to use all we have for his glory. This doesn't mean we have to wander into the most remote recesses of Africa or South America or become a TV evangelist with a national following. Rather, our daily service manifests itself in the details of how we treat the least of God's children.

We serve Jesus daily in whatever place God has put us with whatever talents God has given us. It is the small, everyday ways we serve Jesus and his broken children that keep us ready for Jesus' return. For the faithful, the devil isn't in the details; God is..

[Jim Carlen] liked to have his fingers in everything.
— *Former UVA sports information director Eddie Barrett*

'Don't sweat the small stuff' doesn't apply in our faith life; nothing we do for Jesus is small stuff.

DAY 92

THE FAME GAME

Read 1 Kings 10:1-10, 18-29.

"King Solomon was greater in riches and wisdom than all the other kings of the earth. The whole world sought audience with Solomon" (vv. 23-24).

She played long before the women's game received the media exposure it does today. Nevertheless, Georgeann Wells is the most famous player in West Virginia women's basketball history.

Wells' fame doesn't come from her career, though she was successful. Playing at WVU from 1983-86, she was a four-year letter winner, the team captain as a senior, a freshman All-America in 1983, and a third-team All-America in 1985. She still holds the school career record for blocked shots.

No, Wells' lasting game comes from what she did in one game.

A 6-7 center, Wells decided she would dunk in a game. Each day after practice, she spent extra time working with the coaches solely on dunking. She often dunked up to twenty times in a day to perfect her form and to gain the maximum leverage from her height. In the 1983-84 season, she dunked against Massachusetts, but it was waved off because of a foul call elsewhere on the floor.

But then on Dec. 21, 1984, against Charleston, Georgeann Wells made women's basketball history. With West Virginia comfortably ahead, she "took a full-court pass from Lisa Ribble and soared to the basket for a one-handed stuff." She was the first women's college basketball player to dunk in a game.

The dunk made Wells an instant celebrity. It appeared on network television; *Sports Illustrated* wrote about it. She was the guest of honor at a luncheon in New York City. It earned her a display in the Naismith Basketball Hall of Fame.

Have you ever wanted to be famous like Georgeann Wells? Hanging out with other rich and famous people, having folks with microphones listen to what you say, throwing money around like toilet paper, meeting adoring and clamoring fans, signing autographs, and posing for the paparazzi before you climb into your imported sports car?

Many of us yearn to be famous, well-known in the places and by the people that we believe matter. That's all fame amounts to: strangers knowing your name and your face.

The truth is that you are already famous where it really does matter, which excludes TV's talking heads, screaming teenagers, rapt moviegoers, or D.C. power brokers. You are famous because Almighty God knows your name, your face, and everything else there is to know about you.

If a persistent photographer snapped you pondering this fame — the only kind that has eternal significance — would the picture show the world unbridled joy or the shell-shocked expression of a mug shot?

Unmatched until 1994, [Georgeann Wells'] feat is still one of the sport's most talked about accomplishments.
— 'The History of WVU Women's Basketball'

**You're already famous because God knows
your name and your face, which may be either
reassuring or terrifying.**

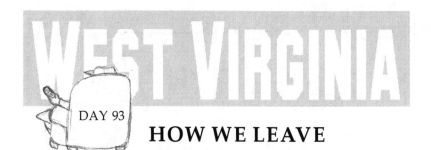

HOW WE LEAVE

Read 2 Kings 2:1-12.

"A chariot of fire and horses of fire appeared and separated the two of them, and Elijah went up to heaven in a whirlwind" (v. 11).

Hall-of-fame football coach Clarence Spears wasn't fired, wasn't dissatisfied, and was offered a substantial raise. So why did he leave WVU? A chance to work at a major medical facility.

From 1921-24, Spears led the Mountaineers to glory with a 30-6-3 record. He was a taskmasker who believed in conditioning. He required his WVU teams to run 25 minutes before breakfast at training camp. He did not, however, believe in scrimmaging. "We had little full-powered body contact," he said. "Only once a week."

Spears weighted close to 300 pounds and detested his nickname, "Fats." "I had a terrible inferiority complex except when I was on the football field," he once said. "When I was 14 years old, I weighed about 214 pounds. That took a lot of clothes."

Just how sensitive he was about his weight was illustrated at a fundraising event in Huntington for which he was the guest speaker. The toastmaster mentioned Spears' "rotund" figure in his introduction. "Visibly irritated," the coach "rose and took a bow in recognition of the applause." Then, instead of stepping up to the rostrum to speak, he sat back down "so emphatically that everyone in the room understood" he was not going to speak. An eloquent speaker, alumni secretary Roy Yoke gamely filled in. It was twenty years before the athletic department could organize another fundraising event in Huntington.

After the 1924 season, Minnesota called with an offer that matched the one WVU athletic director Harry Stansbury had made: a 10-year contract at $15,000 per year. But Minnesota had something West Virginia couldn't match: the famed Mayo Clinic. The school "sweetened the deal" by allowing Spears to work there.

With every stop in his coaching years aimed at advancing his medical career, Spears left.

Unlike Clarence Spears and WVU, we can't always choose how we leave. Sometimes circumstances beyond our control force a move. A job transfer or an untenable situation at work. An elderly parent needed care.

Sometimes the only choice we have about leaving is the manner in which we go, whether we depart with style and grace or not. Our exit from life is the same way. Unless we usurp God's authority over life and death, we can't choose how we die, just how we handle it. Perhaps the most frustrating aspect of dying is that we have at most very little control over the process. As with our birth, our death is in God's hands. We finally must surrender to his will even if we have spent a lifetime refusing to do so.

We do, however, control our destination. How we leave isn't up to us; where we spend eternity is — and that depends on our relationship with Jesus.

The possibilities for my medical career at Minnesota were too good to turn down, so I left.
— *Clarence Spears on why he left WVU*

How you go isn't up to you; where you go is.

DAY 94

STOP, THIEF!

Read Exodus 22:1-15.

"A thief must certainly make restitution" (v. 2b).

Karl Joseph caught more passes than the entire Georgia Southern team did. That doesn't sound too unusual considering Southern is a ground-oriented team. Except that Joseph was a safety.

The Mountaineers hosted the defending Sun Belt Conference champions in the 2015 season opener. The WVU offense certainly did its part. Junior quarterback Skyler Howard was 16-for-25 passing for 359 yards and two touchdowns. Freshman wide receiver Jovon Durante caught three passes for 121 yards and a touchdown. The run game added 188 yards from Rushel Shell, Wendell Smallwood, Donte Thomas-Williams, and back up QB William Crest.

The collective star of the night, however, was the Mountaineer defense, which pitched a shutout in the 44-0 romp. It was the first WVU shutout of a major-college team since the 38-0 whitewashing of Cincinnati in 2005. (The defense would gain a second shutout in 2015 with the 49-0 blanking of Kansas on Nov. 21.) It was also the first time Ga. Southern had been shut out since 1995. The defense limited the Eagles to 195 rushing yards, considerably below the 381 yards-per-game the team averaged in 2014.

The individual star of the defense was Joseph, a senior safety who in the third quarter took thievery to record heights. He intercepted three Southern passes, the first Mountaineer to do that since Vann Washington in 1994's 52-16 defeat of La. Tech. "We shoot to get three takeaways as a defense," said senior safety KJ Dillon. "He got three by himself."

Joseph also led the team with eight tackles. He had a hand in a fourth turnover, scooping up a fumble on a bungled option pitch.

And, yes, Joseph caught more of Southern's passes than their receivers did. The Eagles had only two completions. His reaction to the news was to laugh out loud at how silly the stat sounded.

There was nothing silly, however, about his legal thievery.

Buckle up your seat belt. Wear a bicycle or motorcycle helmet. Use your pooper scooper to clean up after your dog. Don't walk on the grass. Picky ordinances, picky laws — in all their great abundance, they're an inescapable part of our modern lives.

When Moses came stumbling down Mt. Sinai after spending time as God's secretary, he brought with him a whole mess of laws and regulations, many of which undoubtedly seem picky to us today. What some of them provide, though, are practical examples of what for God is the basic principle underlying the theft of personal property: what is wrong must be made right.

While most of us today won't have to worry too much about the theft of livestock such as oxen, sheep, and donkeys, making what is wrong right remains a way of life for Christians. To get right with other people requires anything from restitution to apologies. To get right with God requires Jesus Christ.

That's amazing, and that's all I can say.
— KJ Dillon on Karl Joseph's three interceptions vs. Ga. Southern

To make right the wrong of stealing requires restitution; to make right our relationship with God requires Jesus Christ.

DAY 95

THE END

Read Revelation 22:7-17.

*"I am the Alpha and the Omega, the First and the Last,
the Beginning and the End" (v. 13).*

After thirty seasons as a head coach, Don Nehlen decided it was time to retire. He wanted to end his career with a victory, but it sure didn't seem likely.

One Sunday night in October of 2000, the WVU head coach was driving home from another full day of watching film when he suddenly realized a few things. He would be 65 in January, he had been coming home late on Sundays for 43 years, and — most importantly — he didn't love his job as he once had.

When he got home, he told his wife, Merry Ann, "Mac, I'm going to retire. It's time." She was surprised, but told him it was fine with her if he were sure. The next day, Nehlen called athletic director Ed Pastilong and told him the news. He publicly announced his retirement before the Syracuse game of Nov. 3.

After that, the program degenerated into something resembling chaos. Pastilong named Clemson assistant Rich Rodriguez as Nehlen's successor. Right away, he announced that none of the coaches on Nehlen's staff would be retained.

When WVU landed a berth in the Music City Bowl against a very good Mississippi team, Nehlen wasn't even sure his assistants would hang around to coach the game. Eventually, they decided to make the trip to Nashville out of loyalty, but they were

MOUNTAINEERS

collectively blunt in saying they really didn't want to do it. Their interest lay in lining up another job to support their families.

Nehlen said the practices leading up to the bowl game were "miserable." "We had lousy practices and lousy meetings," he said. "Things didn't look good."

But on the game's second play, fullback Wes Ours turned a short pass into a 40-yard touchdown. Ole Miss never recovered. The Mountaineers roared to a 49-9 lead, and the man coaching his last game ordered his coaches to substitute freely.

Nehlen ended his career with an impressive 49-38 win.

One of life's basic truths is that everything ends. Even the stars have a life cycle, though admittedly it's rather lengthy. Erosion eventually will wear a boulder to a pebble. Life itself is temporary; all living things have a beginning and an end.

Within the framework of our own lifetimes, we all experience endings. Loved ones, friends, and pets die; relationships fracture; jobs dry up; our health, clothes, lawn mowers, TV sets — they all wear out. Even this world as we know it will end.

One of the greatest ironies of God's gift of life is that not even death is immune from the great truth that all things must end. That's because through Jesus' life, death, and resurrection, God himself acted to end any power death once had over life.

Because of Jesus, the end of life has ended. God's eternity — which is outside time and has no end — is ours for the claiming.

It's time to let somebody else go home at 11 o'clock and let me sit at home and watch games on television.
— Don Nehlen as he decided it was time to retire

Everything ends; thanks to Jesus, so does death.

NOTES
(by Devotion Day Number)

1   In 1891, two WVU students . . . played football at Yale.: John Antonik, *West Virginia University Football Vault* (Atlanta: Whitman Publishing, LLC, 2009), p. 9.

1   A production of Richard III generated $160: Antonik, *West Virginia University Football Vault*, p. 9.

1   The money was used to . . . and a rule book.: Tony Constantine with Don Miller, *Mountaineer Football 1891-1969* (Morgantown: Athletic Publicity Office West Virginia University, 1969), p. 3.

1   the squad from Pennsylvania . . . seasons under its belt.: Antonik, *West Virginia University Football Vault*, p. 11.

1   The visitors made the . . . Morgantown by steamboat.: Constantine with Miller, *Mountaineer Football 1891-1969*, p. 3.

1   At 3 p.m.: Antonik, *West Virginia University Football Vault*, p. 11.

1   Rain turned to snow . . . stood in the mud: Antonik, *West Virginia University Football Vault*, p. 11.

2   It was a game no one expected West Virginia's football team to win.": Stefanie Loh, "Un-bowl-ievable," *Believe* (Morgantown: *The Dominion Post*, 2008), p. 139.

2   it was dubbed the "Miracle in the Desert.": Antonik, *West Virginia University Football Vault*, p. 136.

2   "thought to be unstable . . . loss in school history.": Drew Rubenstein, "Stewart Deserves a Serious Look," *Believe* (Morgantown: *The Dominion Post*, 2008), p. 157.

2   No school "with a . . won a bowl game.": Rubenstein, "Stewart Deserves," p. 157.

2   "no one gave West Virginia a chance against the powerful Sooners.": Antonik, *West Virginia University Football Vault*, p. 135.

2   "They never stopped believing,": Loh, "Un-bowl-evable," p. 139.

2   West Virginia pulled off the most improbable victory in school history.: Antonik, *West Virginia University Football Vault*, p. 137.

3   At the time, many schools . . . to carry the games: John Antonik, *Roll out the Carpet* (Morgantown: West Virginia University Press, 2010), p. 31.

3   head coach Dyke Raese . . . get in to his players.: Antonik, *Roll out the Carpet*, p. 33.

3   "When they won, it was total. . . began wiring them some funds.: Antonik, *Roll out the Carpet*, p. 33.

3   We had all gone . . . going to the tournament.: Antonik, *Roll out the Carpet*, p. 31.

4   "I felt like they felt . . . make them regret it.": Todd Murray, "WVU RB Smallwood Exacts Revenge on Terps," *TheDPost.com*, Sept. 26, 2015, http://thedpost.com/Smallwood-exacts-re--venge-on-Te.

4   As he met the press . . . then he winked.: Joey Lomonaco, "WVU Trounces Terrapins, 45-6," *The DPost.com*, Sept. 26, 2015, http://thedpost.com/WVU-trounces-Terrap--ins,-45-6.

4   to credit to coincidence . . . to underestimate Holgorsen.": Lomonaco, "WVU Trounces Terrapins 45-6."

4   Dana Holgerson expunged the most sullying spot on his resume.: Lomonaco, "WVU Trounces Terrapins 45-6."

5   Twenty-seven persons, including . . . prepare for the game.: Antonik, *West Virginia University Football Vault*, p. 29.

5   the Mountaineers wilted in the heat and the sandy field they were playing on.: Constantine with Miller, *Mountaineer Football 1891-1969*, p. 25.

5   The squad didn't arrive home . . . Pike's Peak and Chicago.: Antonik, *West Virginia University Football Vault*, p. 29.

6   "We came into the . . . a reasonably low scoring game,": John Antonik, *The Backyard Brawl* (Morgantown: West Virginia University Press, 2012), p. 89.

6   "We were leading 21-0 and . . . "What a mistake that was.": Antonik, *The Backyard Brawl*, p. 87.

6   Corum was led to declare . . . had to see to believe.: Antonik, *The Backyard Brawl*, p. 89.

6   When a Western Union . . .quit drinking during games.: Antonik, *The Backyard Brawl*, p. 95.

6   They then called Morgantown to personally verify the score.: Mickey Furfari, "Dunlevy Was an Outstanding Receiver at WVU, " *The Times West Virginian*, July 22, 2015, http://www.times wv.com/sports/furfari-column-dunlevy-was-an-outstanding-receiver-at-wvu/article_0b95d658.

6   A WVU assistant coach scouting . . . "Please send corrected score.": Antonik, *The Backyard Brawl*, pp. 95-96.

6   "I've never seen a game like it in my life,": Antonik, *The Backyard Brawl*, p. 89.

6   It seems unbelievable that a team scoring 48 points could lose.: Antonik, *The Backyard Brawl*, p. 89.

7   a Hawaii fan sitting . . . under his own power.: Chris Mascaro, "Brawl Breaks Out," *SI.com*, Nov. 18, 2013, http://www.si.com/si-wire/2013/11/18/brawl-breaks-out-at-hawaii-west-virginia-

7   I saw the fight break . . . with something in the back.: Mascaro, "Brawl Breaks Out."
8   The head man's dad, . . . them on the sidelines.: John Antonik, "WVU Football: A Band of Brothers," *WVUsports.com*, June 30, 2016, http://www.wvusports.com/page. cfm?story= 30379&cat=football.
8   Ka'Raun White admitted to benefits . . . trust more than your brother?": Antonik, "WVU Football."
8   It's pretty cool that we have a bunch of brothers here.: Antonik, "WVU Football."
9   *Sports Illustrated* chronicled Lewis' . . . wins over Pitt in 1952 and '53.: Antonik, *The Backyard Brawl*, p. 48.
10 When Nehlen told Bo . . . 15 of those guys a year.": Antonik, *The Backyard Brawl*, p. 160.
10 Nehlen walked in and . . . them both to the floor.: Antonik, *The Backyard Brawl*, p. 160.
10 Right then we realized it was going to be a different regime.: Antonik, *The Backyard Brawl*, p. 160.
11 Students camped outside the . . . the student section was full.: Antonik, *Roll Out the Carpet*, p. 186.
11 "was taking his team into an . . . as he unsuccessfully tried to sleep.: Antonik, *Roll Out the Carpet*, p. 185.
11 How did you ever talk me into coming here to play, Gale?: Antonik, *Roll Out the Carpet*, p. 185.
12 "It was hard to get . . . in the seventh grade.: Thayer Evans, "Holgorsen's Long But Tumultuous Journey," *FOXSports*, Sept. 23, 2011, http://msn.foxsports.com/collegefootball/story/west-virginia-mountaineers-coach-dana-holgorsen.
12 he "toiled in obscurity" at . . . was brief. "Come here," he said.: Evans, "Holgorsen's Long But Tumultuous Journey."
12 At OSU, he lived in a hotel . . . waiting for when Bill Stewart left.: Evans, "Holgorsen's Long But Tumultuous Journey."
12 It was bad football, a bunch of slow little white kids running around.: Evans, "Holgorsen's Long But Tumultuous Journey."
13 *ESPN*'s Ivan Maisel credited Harris with being the player who turned West Virginia into a national program.: Antonik, *The Backyard Brawl*, p. 200.
13 At a press conference in February . . . "I had no money," he said.: Antonik, *The Backyard Brawl*, p. 199.
13 He saw other players . . . are basically following suit,": Antonik, *The Backyard Brawl*, p. 200.
13 "You've got people in . . . that when you're young.": Antonik, *The Backyard Brawl*, p. 200.
13 "Looking back on it," he . . . I did it was wrong.: Antonik, *The Backyard Brawl*, p. 199.
13 The one thing I regret . . . he thought about [my turning pro].": Antonik, *The Backyard Brawl*, p. 200.
13 Leaving school early was a mistake [Major] Harris still regrets.: Antonik, *The Backyard Brawl*, p. 199.
14 his first two snaps were . . . snaps on their chests.": John Antonik, "2006: Sugar Bowl: Dan Mozes," *WVUsports.com*, http://www.wvusports.com/blogs/cfm?blog=footballBlog&story=28140.
14 On the play Rodriguez called . . . for a first down.: Antonik, "2006 Sugar Bowl: Dan Mozes."
14 "probably ended up winning it for the Mountaineers.": Antonik, "2006 Sugar Bowl: Dan Mozes."
15 Quarterback Dan Kendra knew . . . a shot what the heck?": Antonik, *The Backyard Brawl*, p. 132.
15 By the time McKenzie's boot . . . I was going to die,": Antonik, *The Backyard Brawl*, p. 134.
15 Smith went onto the field . . . gave a student his glasses.: Antonik, *The Backyard Brawl*, pp. 134-35.
15 I got a copy of the highlight . . . giving the kid his glasses.: Antonik, *The Backyard Brawl*, p. 135.
16 He dribbled the ball behind . . . lob pass from a teammate.: This series of Hot Rod Hundley's crowd-pleasing antics is found at Antonik, *Roll Out the Carpet*, p. 64, and "Hot Rod Hundley," *Wikipedia, the free encyclopedia*, https://en.wikipedia.org/wiki/Hot_Rod_Hundley.
16 Against William & Mary in . . . he scored on a layup.: Antonik, *Roll Out the Carpet*, p. 83.
16 He sometimes led the crowd . . . taken out of a game.: Antonik, *Roll Out the Carpet*, p. 75.
16 He often acknowledged applause during a game.: Antonik, *Roll Out the Carpet*, p. 70.
16 the more he received the . . . work. He was a nut,": Antonik, *Roll Out the Carpet*, p. 64.
16 To [Hot Rod] Hundley, basketball . . . fans across the state.: Roland Lazenby, *Jerry West* (New York: Ballentine Books, 2009), p. 117.
17 "the tensest game I've ever been in.": Todd Murray, "Mountaineers Hold Off BYU," *The Dominion Post*, Sept 24, 2016, http://www.thedpost.com/mountaineers-hold-off-byu-in-thr.
17 he "kind of threw a . . . players to stay ready: Murray, "Mountaineers Hold off BYU."
17 A lot of things happened that put that victory in jeopardy.: Murray, "Mountaineers Hold off BYU."
18 By 1975, the good old days . . . in the rearview mirror.": Antonik, *The Backyard Brawl*, p. 145.
18 That's the year WVU . . . the facility was falling down.: Antonik, *The Backyard Brawl*, p. 145.
18 The Astroturf was "terrible . . . weight room at the time.: Antonik, *The Backyard Brawl*, p. 145.
18 The weight room was so . . . "It was like a dungeon.": Antonik, *The Backyard Brawl*, p. 146.

WEST VIRGINIA

18 "It was like you were . . . York City at night time,": Antonik, *The Backyard Brawl*, p. 147.

18 The team meeting room . . . the field for the meeting.: Antonik, *The Backyard Brawl*, p. 146.

18 We used to call it the snake pit.: Antonik, *The Backyard Brawl*, p. 144.

19 The athletic department had . . . out in a bad way.: Mike Casazza, *Waiting for the Fall* (St. Paul, Minn.: Stance & Speed LLC, 2012), p. 271.

19 "the excitement about a new league . . . rejected and depressed the next.": Casazza, *Waiting for the Fall*, p. 273.

19 It seems a U.S. senator . . . invited and accepted WVU.: Casazza, *Waiting for the Fall*, p. 274.

19 League honchos suddenly . . . was finally all over.: Casazza, *Waiting for the Fall*, p. 275.

19 The Mountaineers were merely . . . to find a new home.: Casazza, *Waiting for the Fall*, p. 271.

20 Thrasher wanted to be a figure . . . shooting became a passion.: Rick Maese, "Ginny Thrasher Picked Up a Gun," *The Washington Post*, Aug. 6, 2016, http://www.washingtonpost.com/sports/olympics/ginny-thrasher-picked-up-a-gun.

20 she "wasn't considered a . . . experienced shooters in the field.": Maese, "Ginny Thrasher."

20 landing about twenty hours . . . with an 8:30 a.m. physics class.: Maese, "Ginny Thrasher."

20 This is beyond my wildest dreams.: Maese, "Ginny Thrasher."

21 At the time, the average . . . a mere two and a half years.: Antonik, *West Virginia University Football Vault*, p. 56.

21 But he was familiar with . . . He was offered the job.: Antonik, *West Virginia University Football Vault*, p. 59.

21 Lewis' legend took on mythical . . . board game was named after him.: Antonik, *West Virginia University Football Vault*, p. 61.

21 I always will feel that . . . But I fooled them.: Antonik, *West Virginia University Football Vault*, p. 58.

22 "I'm not going to lie to . . . "That hurt. It really did.": Casazza, *Waiting for the Fall*, p. 281.

22 a "punch in the face.": Casazza, *Waiting for the Fall*, p. 281.

22 watched in dismay as . . . however, corral the ball.: Casazza, *Waiting for the Fall*, pp. 281-82.

22 The guy on the team with one good hand got the ball?; Casazza, *Waiting for the Fall*, p. 282.

23 "Football definitely saved my life,": Martin Frank, "Delaware Native Wendell Smallwood: 'Football Saved My Life,'" *The News Journal*, July 22, 2016, http://www.delawareonline.com/story/sports/nfl/eagles/2016/07/22/delaware-native-wendell-smallwood-football-saved-my-lfe/87443314/.

23 Football, he said, gave him . . . he would be OK.: Frank, "Delaware Native Wendell Smallwood."

23 Many kids on [my] teams . . . [not] for recreation.: Frank, "Delaware Native Wendell Smallwood."

24 "slightly radioactive. . . . I knew I would coach again,": Dan Wetzel, "W.Va. Coach Huggins Keeps Bouncing Back," *YAHOO!Sports*, May 26, 2010, http://rivals.yahoo.com/ncaa/basketball/news.

24 The guy has fallen down more . . . gotten back up and kept coaching.: Wetzel, "W.Va. Coach Huggins Keeps Bouncing Back."

25 Nehlen, that new coach, sat on a platform . . . Jay Rockefeller and John Denver.: Don Nehlen with Shelly Poe, *Tales from the West Virginia Mountaineers Sideline* (New York City: Sports Publishing, 2012), p. 57.

25 Looking for some kind of . . . they went stark raving nuts.: Nehlen with Poe, *Tales from the West Virginia Mountaineers Sideline*, pp. 59-60.

25 "I think that about 11 Mountaineers leapt in the air to intercept the football,": Nehlen with Poe, *Tales from the West Virginia Mountaineers Sideline*, p. 61.

25 I could not believe how real . . . players thought so, too.: Nehlen with Poe, *Tales from the West Virginia Mountaineers Sideline*, p. 60.

26 Healed up by season's . . . one season of eligibility,": Mickey Furfari, "Kinder First of Only Two Ever to Wear 100 on Jersey," *Bluefield Daily Telegraph*, Sept. 24, 2013, http://www.bdtonline.com/sports/sports_columns/kinder-first-of-only-two-ever-to-wear-on-jersey/article.

26 In 1963, Kinder asked the . . . publicity wearing No. 100,": Mickey Furfari, "WVU Kicker Wore No. 100 Proudly," *The Register-Herald*, March 27, 2013, http://www.register-herald.com/todays sportsfront/x1485886137/WVU-kicker-wore-No-100-proudly.

26 I just didn't realize it was the state's birthday.: Furfari, " WVU Kicker Wore No. 100 Proudly."

27 When quarterback guru Steve . . . had become damaged goods." Jake Trotter, "From Seventh-Grade Phenom to Failed QB to Elite Receiver," *ESPN.com*, Oct. 6, 2017, http://www.espn.com/college-football/story/_/id/20923614/west-virginia-david-sillos-7th-grad-phenom-failed-qb-elite-receiver.

27 We thought about [Sills . . . anybody look like that.: Trotter, "From Seventh-Grade Phenom."

28 "One of the most famous shots in the history of WVU basketball": Angelica Trinone, "Father and Son Share Success on the Court," *WValways*, Jan. 29, 2016, http://www.wvalways.com/story31095993/father-and-son-share-success-on-the-court.

28   a Cincinnati player verified . . . teammate got "a piece of it.": Antonik, *Roll Out the Carpet*, p. 205.

28   one lobbed a dead fish . . . was shooting a free throw.: Antonik *Roll Out the Carpet*, p. 147.

28   The final game of the . . . to check out the arena.: Antonik, *Roll Out the Carpet*, p. 199.

28   Bowling Green's Dan Dakich was . . . Ohio and his old job.: Antonik, *Roll Out the Carpet*, p. 210.

29   Senior cornerback David Lockwood noted . . . never anything like that.": Patrick Southern, "A Storied History," *The DAonline.com*, Oct. 3, 2008, http://www.thedaonline.com/article_461a3063.

30   "one of the most bizarre finishes in Backyard Brawl history.": Antonik, *The Backyard Brawl*, p. 5.

30   "What player or coach . . . scored a touchdown,": Antonik, *The Backyard Brawl*, p. 5.

30   My difficult job had now become impossible.: Antonik, *The Backyard Brawl*, p. 5.

31   "Everyone knew that once . . . he was going to be special.": Craig Meyer, "No Standing Pat," *Pittsburgh Post-Gazette*, http://newsineractive.post-gazette.com/oral-history/west-virginia/.

31   After that game, White called . . . a pro baseball career.: Meyer, "No Standing Pat."

31   I was almost ready to give up and give in.: Meyer, "No Standing Pat."

32   Head coach Bill Kern surprisingly . . . quickly accepted it.: Antonik, *The Backyard Brawl*, p. 19.

32   Empty seats and frigid temperatures greeted the teams,: Antonik, *The Backyard Brawl*, p. 22.

32   He thought he had fallen . . . not in the end zone.: Antonik, *The Backyard Brawl*, p. 22.

32   The ball scooted on the . . . a chair at the fan: Antonik, *The Backyard Brawl*, p. 23.

32   The press box crew dispatched . . . during all that confusion.: Antonik, *The Backyard Brawl*, p. 25.

32   The goal posts were going . . . game ended 17–0.: Antonik, *The Backyard Brawl*, p. 23.

33   "The most famous athlete to ever wear the Gold and Blue,": John Antonik, "WVU Sports Hall of Fame: Jerry West," *WVUsports.com*, http://www.wvusports.com/hallOfFame.cfm?func=viewProfile&hofID=49.

33   "We never ever went anyplace . . . We didn't have the money.": Lazenby, *Jerry West*, p. 115.

33   West arrived in Morgantown . . . started walking the tracks.: Lazenby, *Jerry West*, p. 114.

33   Akers called head coach Fred . . . West to return to campus.: Lazenby, *Jerry West*, p. 115.

33   West's salvation that first year . . . [and] found a little comfort.": Lazenby, *Jerry West*, p. 115-16.

33   I was terribly disillusioned by being away from home.: Lazenby, *Jerry West*, p. 114.

34   "the greatest bowl victory . . . in WVU football history.": "Double Life," *wvutoday*, Dec. 23, 2009, http://wvutoday.wvu.edu/n/2009/12/23/double-life.

34   There he stood with his . . . when I put it on.": Stefanie Loh, "Williams Creates a Scene," *Believe: The Story of the 2007 West Virginia Mountaineer Football Team* (Morgantown: The Dominion Post, 2008), p. 71.

34   "a little fat boy. . . . I looked like Bobby Hill.": Chuck Finder, "Chunky Child Has Grown into Leader," *Pittsburgh Post-Gazette*, Oct. 14, 2007, http://www.post-gazette.com/sports/wvu/2007/10/14/Chunky-child-has-grown-into-leader-of-West-Virginia-s-stingy-defense/stories/200710140175.

35   Amos was born in Ivory . . . wanted to see it through,": Marty Burns, "Amos Zereoue West Virginia's Fast-Forward Sophomore Tailback," *Sports Illustrated*, Oct. 6, 1997, http://www.si.com/vault/1997/10/06/232764/amos-zereoue-west-virginias-fast-forward-sophomore-tailback.

35   I knew my father was right.: Burns, "Amos Zereoue West Virginia's Fast-Forward Sophomore."

36   "I should have consulted . . . I was ignorant.": Andy Staples, "Centered by Fatherhood, Will Grier Is Enjoying the Final Year of His Winding College Career," *SI.com*, Oct. 30, 2018, https://www.si.com/college-football/2018-10-30/will-grier-family-daughter-west-virginia-mountaineers.

36   The previous January, Grier . . . Before long, they were inseparable: Staples, "Centered by Fatherhood."

36   He now had two guides . . . I'm in a good spot.: Staples, "Centered by Fatherhood."

36   [Having a family] gives you . . . It's not just you.: Staples, "Centered by Fatherhood."

37   Waco was in the grips . . . to Morgantown Monday morning: Mike Casazza, "Man of the (Early) Hour," *Charleston Gazette-Mail*, March 3, 2014, http://blogs.wvgazettemail.com/wvu/2014/03/03/man-of-the-hour-mike-carey/.

37   Sometimes [the] obstacles come after the success.: Casazza, "Man of the (Early) Hour."

38   WVU's "undersized" quarterback: Bob Hertzel, "Howard Shows His Toughness in Opener," *The Exponent Telegram*, Sept. 3, 2016, http://www.theet.com/sports/wvu/howard-shows-his-toughness-in-opener/article.

38   "a shot to the rib . . . vibrating like [a] xylophone.": Hertzel, "Howard Shows His Toughness."

38   He slowly returned to the . . . going down in pain.: Mike Casazza, "WVU Football Opens with Win Against Missouri," *Charleston Gazette-Mail*, Sept. 3, 2016, http://www.wvgazettemail.com/sports/wvu/20160903/wvu-football-opens-with-win-against-missouri.

38   "the situation seemed dark.": Hertzel, "Howard Shows His Toughness."

38   "Hey, I'm a ball player," . . . Let's try it again.": Hertzel, "Howard Shows His Toughness."

38   He's a tough kid. . . . would question his toughness.: Hertzel, "Howard Shows His Toughness."

39   "one of the greatest quarterbacks in Mountaineer history.": "Fred Wyant," *Wikipedia, the free encyclopedia*, https://en.wikipedia.org/wiki/Fred_Wyant.

39   "was the only good player . . . the 25 and then to midfield.: Antonik, *The Backyard Brawl*, p. 32.

39   "Look, it's your last game and . . . huddle slowly came around.: Antonik, *The Backyard Brawl*, p. 33.

39   It was like a light bulb went off.: Antonik, *The Backyard Brawl*, p. 33.

40   He quickly gave way to . . . a whole lot about soccer,": John Antonik, "WVU Men's Soccer Turns 50," *MSNSportsNET.com*, Aug. 30, 2010, http://wvutoday.wvu.edu/n/2010/08/30/wvu-men-s-soccer-turns-50.

40   A field on the outskirts . . . best that we could": Antonik, "WVU Men's Soccer Turns 50."

40   We started off on a small scale.: Antonik, "WVU Men's Soccer Turns 50."

41   Juskowich recalled that it . . . to be on scholarship.": Antonik, *The Backyard Brawl*, p. 107.

41   many of the fans "were . . . down below the field.": Antonik, *The Backyard Brawl*, p. 108.

41   People don't make decisions like that anymore.: Antonik, *The Backyard Brawl*, p. 107.

42   Cook crossed the goal . . . a girl. I apologize.": "West Virginia Routs Clemson," *ESPN.com*, Jan. 4, 2012, http://cdn.espn.com/ncf/recap?gameId=320040228.

42   "If you watched more . . . outplayed, point-blank, period,": Heather Dinich, "Clemson Collapses on ACC's Biggest Stage," *ESPN.com*, Jan. 5, 2012, http://www.espn.com/blog/acc/post/_/id/35295/clemson-collapses-on-accs-biggest-stage.

42   Am I embarrassed?" Definitely. . . . getting beat like that.: Dinich, "Clemson Collapses."

43   Quarterback Jeff Hostetler calmly . . . to go. Let's do it!": Antonik, *The Backyard Brawl*, p. 178.

43   "It was one of those things . . . as the stadium exploded.": Antonik, *The Backyard Brawl*, p. 179.

43   We knew after pounding, pounding and pounding . . . that it was there.: Antonik, *The Backyard Brawl*, p. 179.

44   Robinson was a well-liked . . . the president," Harlow answered. "Oh,": Antonik, *Roll Out the Carpet*, p. 149.

44   With the score tied . . . the truth around here.: Antonik, *Roll Out the Carpet*, pp. 149-50.

45   "the experts, the pundits, and even the fans were underwhelmed.": Casazza, *Waiting for the Fall*, p. 22.

45   the Big East had a "bruised . . . merit a spot in the BCS.: Casazza, *Waiting for the Fall*, p. 22.

45   "too young, too small, and too underrecruited": Casazza, *Waiting for the Fall*, p. 23.

45   "No one likes to hear they can't win or don't belong,": Casazza, *Waiting for the Fall*, p. 23.

45   It may have been the best thing to happen to them.: Casazza, *Waiting for the Fall*, p. 23.

46   "We're playing on national . . . dominate in doing so.": Jeff Toquinto, "From the Bench: 25 Years Later," *connectBridgeport.com*, Aug. 4, 2013, http://www.connect-bridgeport.com/connect.cfm?func=view&section=Sports-Blog&item=From-the-Bench-25-Years-Later-Major-Harris.

46   "the apex of my career." . . . "tops for me.": Toquinto, "From the Bench: 25 Years Later."

46   Hurrying his team to . . . the team went left.: John Antonik, "30 Most Unforgettable Games," *WVUsports.com*, July 25, 2010, http://www.wvusports.com/30Games.cfm?story=16786.

46   "He faked out the entire . . . run in school history.": Tara Curtis, "Hall of Famer and WVU Great Major Harris to Lead Homecoming Parade," *WVUtoday.edu*, Oct. 14, 2010, http://wvutoday.wvu.edu/n/2010/10/14/hall-of-famer-and-wvu-great-major-harris.

46   To this day it was . . . in college football history.: Antonik, "30 Most Unforgettable Games."

46   'My fault, coach.' 'I think I can live with it.': Ralph Wiley, "Major Harris Rose From Pittsburgh's Hill District to Football Heights," *SI.com*, Dec. 19, 1988, http://www.si.com/vault/1988/12/19/119089/showdown-in-the-fiesta-bowl.

47   "kids are lost to the . . . passion to play sports.": Jake Trotter, "Rasul Douglas' Journey to Becoming the Big 12's Best DB," *ESPN.com*, Nov. 17, 2016, http://www.espn.com/college-football/story/_/id/18070582/west-virginia-mountaineers-rasul-douglas-journey-become-big-12-best-db.

47   When Nassau Community College . . . and did the work.: Trotter, "Rasul Douglas' Journey."

47   That was probably the hardest part of my life, for sure.: Trotter, "Rasul Douglas' Journey."

48   "It was like a movie," that unfolded in slow motion.: "WVU Escapes," *ESPN.com*, March 12, 2016, http://cdn.espn.com/ncb/recap?gameId=400870832.

48   "Championship game, main character . . . like, 'Is this possible?'": "WVU Escapes."

48   "Nah, that' didn't count," . . . give the game to us.": "WVU Escapes."

48   Time wasn't on my side, I guess.: "WVU Escapes."

49   "Did he really say that?" . . . show up in the papers: Antonik, *The Backyard Brawl*, p. 71.

49   "I remember when that . . . I was never garbage!": Antonik, *The Backyard Brawl*, p. 72.

49   Late in the game, after . . . beat the garbage men!": Antonik, *The Backyard Brawl*, p. 76.

49   Whoa, ammo!: Antonik, *The Backyard Brawl*, p. 72.

50   "Not every Big 12 game is like this,": "Geno Smith Throws for 656 Yards," *ESPN.go.com*, Sept. 29, 2012, http://scores.espngo.com/.ncf/recap?gameId=32273077.

50   "I might need more gun powder for this game.": Holly Anderson, "Geno Smith, West Virginia Outlast Baylor," *SI.com*, Sept. 30, 2012, http://www.si.com/college-football/campus-union/2012/09/29/west-virginia-baylor-geno-smith-big-12.

51   With a seating capacity of about . . . means of travel at the time.: Antonik, *West Virginia University Football Vault*, p. 29.

51   Stansbury wanted a facility that would seat about 35,000.; Antonik, *West Virginia University Football Vault*, p. 30.

51   The cost was driven . . . Monongahela River be diverted.: Antonik, *West Virginia University Football Vault*, p. 29.

51   The plan was to finance . . . about $100,000 was raised.: Antonik, *West Virginia University Football Vault*, pp. 30, 32.

51   A second campaign was initiated . . . paying off the balance.: Antonik, *West Virginia University Football Vault*, p. 32.

51   It took more than 30 . . . another big-ticket facility project.: Antonik, *West Virginia University Football Vault*, p. 32.

52   "By the time [he] had . . . of the head by a baseball.: Antonik, *Roll Out the Carpet*," p. 106.

52   By Thorn's senior year of . . . to stay in the state.: Antonik, *Roll Out the Carpet*," p. 107.

52   What in the world is this [legislature] thinking about?; Antonik, *Roll Out the Carpet*," p. 107.

53   "Pat came into the . . . size of a grapefruit.": Chuck Finder, "Gator Bowl: West Virginia Rallies to Beat Georgia Tech," *Pittsburgh Post-Gazette*, Jan. 2, 2007, http://www.post-gazette.com/sports/wvu/2007/01/02/Gator-Bowl-West-Virginia-Rallies-to-beat-Georgia-Tech/stories/200701010170.

53   The stadium was bumping. Everything seemed to be clicking.: Finder," Gator Bowl."

54   "I really think [the ACC] . . . had played all along.": Mike Whiteford, "The Road Not Traveled," *The Charleston Gazette*, June 24, 2010, http://www.wvgazette.com/Sports/WVU/201006241018.

54   Roy "Legs" Hawley worked . . . on mostly two-lane roads": Whiteford, "The Road Not Traveled."

54   I really think that . . . into Morgantown hurt us.: Whiteford, "The Road Not Traveled."

55   "nothing short of weird.": Nehlen with Poe, *Tales from the West Virginia Mountaineer Sideline*, p. 1.

55   Nehlen had just returned . . . job at West Virginia,": Nehlen with Poe, *Tales from the West Virginia Mountaineer Sideline*, p. 2.

55   They hit it off until . . . hotel near the airport.: Nehlen with Poe, *Tales from the West Virginia Mountaineer Sideline*, p. 6.

55   When the door to the room . . . they just listened.: Nehlen with Poe, *Tales from the West Virginia Mountaineer Sideline*, p. 7.

55   Nehlen stayed in a high . . . had said of Nehlen, "He's it.": Nehlen with Poe, *Tales from the West Virginia Mountaineer Sideline*, p. 8.

55   I was a little spooked and wondering how anybody knew I was there.: Nehlen with Poe, *Tales from the West Virginia Mountaineer Sideline*, p. 8.

56   "work habits bordered on compulsion." . . . basketball career was barely surviving.": Antonik, *Roll Out the Carpet*, p. 238.

56   Huggins emphasized weight training and strength.: "Joe Alexander," *Wikipedia, the free encyclopedia*, https://en.wikipedia.org/wiki/Joe_Alexander.

56   He gained twenty pounds: "Joe Alexander," *Wikipedia, the free encyclopedia*.

57   dissension among the players . . . it reached the papers.: Antonik, *The Backyard Brawl*, p. 27.

57   a "burly, bushy-browed, mountain of a man,": Antonik, *The Backyard Brawl*, p. 26.

57   At practice, he lined players . . . the survivor was the starter.: Antonik, *The Backyard Brawl*, p. 29.

57   The jubilant players carried . . . all the way to the shower.: Antonik, *The Backyard Brawl*, p. 35.

57   before the kickoff, Pitt . . . with his billy club.: Antonik, *The Backyard Brawl*, p. 35.

57   The well-lubricated West Virginia fan never felt a thing.: Antonik, *The Backyard Brawl*, p. 35.

58   A unique WVU tradition was . . . while chanting "first down.": "Fight Songs and Chants: First Down Cheer," *WVUsports.com*, http://www.wvusports.com/page.cfm?section=13065.

58   Head basketball coach Fred . . . at games since 1978.: Antonik, *Rolling Out the Carpet*, p. 72.

58   It begins when the . . . and greet the Mountaineers!": "Roll Out the Carpet: Let's Roll Out the Carpet!" *WVUsports.com*, http://www.wvusports.com/page.cfm?section=23880.

58   The song has been played at every pre-game show since 1972.: "Country Roads: Take Me Home, Country Roads," *WVUsports.com*, http://www.wvusports.com/page.cfm?section=23881.

58   "a nod to the state's . . . the start of their shift.: "Mountaineer Mantrip," *WVUsports.com*, http://www.wvusports.com/page.cfm?section=21564.

58   The post game: it's a bit of a tear jerker.: Eric Herter, "What a Great Setting for Some Football," *Believe*, p. 10.

59   "the entire West Virginia sideline spilled onto the field, hooting and hollering.": Andrea Adelson, "West Virginia Back in Thick of Big East Race," *ESPN.com*, Nov. 13, 2011, http://www.espn. com/blog/bigeast/post/_/id/26398/west-virginia-back-in-thick-of-big-east-race.

59   Head coach Dana Holgorsen had . . . inevitable times of adversity.: Adelson, "West Virginia Back in Thick."

59   "One word," Geno Smith said. "Pandemonium.": Adelson, "West Virginia Back in Thick."

59   The energy was great. It was great all over the sideline.: Adelson, "West Virginia Back in Thick."

60   "one of the most competitive women I've ever met.": Graham Hays, "Amanda Hill Leans on Brother's Love," *ESPN.com*, Oct. 31, 2012, http://www.espn.com/espnw/news-commentary/article/8568799/espnw-west-virginia-mountaineers-midfielder-amanda-hill-leans-brother-love.

60   Hill's competitive drive was forged . . . "Just [to] make her proud.": Hays, "Amanda Hill Leans on Brother's Love."

60   I feel like I know what she wants me to do, so I just do that.: Hays, "Amanda Hill Leans on Brother's Love."

61   "the greatest all-around athlete in Mountaineer history.": Mickey Furfari, "Rodgers Was Mountaineers' Greatest All-Around Athlete," *The Register-Herald*, March 19, 2013, http://www.register-herald.com/collegesports/x765714564.

61   He had played four years of . . . high school near his home.: Antonik, *West Virginia University Football Vault*, p. 20.

61   he could "throw the . . . has uncovered his name.": Constantine with Miller, *Mountaineer Football 1891-1969*, p. 19.

61   As the 1915 season neared, . . . himself to be kidnapped.: Antonik, *West Virginia University Football Vault*, p. 20.

61   Paul Vance allowed himself . . . not to be Ira Rodgers.: Antonik, *West Virginia University Football Vault*, p. 20.

62   In the spring, Nehlen warned . . . "They'll kill us,": Nehlen with Poe, *Tales from the West Virginia Mountaineers Sideline*, pp. 78-79.

62   he privately told his players . . . certain that they were going to win.": Nehlen with Poe, *Tales from the West Virginia Mountaineers Sideline*, p. 79.

62   With time running out, they kept giving the ball to the fullback.: Nehlen with Poe, *Tales from the West Virginia Mountaineers Sideline*, p. 80.

62   I'm going to try to set a smokescreen for the folks in Oklahoma.: Nehlen with Poe, *Tales from the West Virginia Mountaineers Sideline*, p. 78.

63   when he moved from defensive . . . he liked the offense.: Ben Glicksman, "The Evolution of West Virginia WR and NFL Draft Prospect Kevin White," *Sports Illustrated*, Nov. 19, 2014, http://www.si.com/college-football/2014/11/19/kevin-white-west-virginia-mountaineers.

63   I just made up my mind and said I'm gonna made it happen.: Glicksman, "The Evolution."

64   Huggins had intended to . . . him to take the shot,": "Tarik Phillip's Clutch 3 Seals Win," *ESPN.com*, March 21, 2015, http://cdn.espn.com/ncb/recap?gameId=400785436.

64   My absentmindedness prbably won the game.: "Tarik Phillip's Clutch 3 Seals Win."

65   "a very good high school . . . Schmitt and his mother.: Casazza, *Waiting for the Fall*, p. 72.

65   showed up at the Puskar . . . a place to play.: John Antonik, "2006 Sugar Bowl: Owen Schmitt," *WVUSports.com*, http://www.wvusports.com/page.cfm?story=28160.

65   Schmitt and halfback Steve . . . fullbacks in the nation.: "Owen Schmitt," *Wikipedia, the free encyclopedia*, https://en.wikipedia.org/wiki/Owen_Schmidt.

65   He was tagged the "Runaway . . . every three games he played.: Antonik, "2006 Sugar Bowl: Owen Schmitt."

65   He couldn't shake the feeling he was capable of doing so much more.: Casazza, *Waiting for the Fall*, p. 72.

66   "one of the greatest special . . . punter in school history.": Ken Durbin, "16 — Todd Sauerbrun," *West Virginia 100 Day Countdown to Victory*, Aug 16, 2012, http://wvu100countdown.blogspot.com/2012/08/16-todd-sauerbrun.html.

66   Quarterback Chad Johnston laughingly . . . ended practice right then.": Antonik, *The Backyard Brawl*, p. 214.

66   Nehlen had a strict rule . . . told that story a lot.: Antonik, *The Backyard Brawl*, p. 215.

66   That was just Todd.: Antonik, *The Backyard Brawl*, p. 214.

67   The rotund coach was always . . . threw him over a fence.: Antonik, *West Virginia University Football Vault*, p. 34.

67   With one game left . . . games of [Nardacci's] career," Constantine with Miller, *Mountaineer Football 1981-1969*, p. 31.

198

68 One player thought a press . . . the shot wasn't any good.: "The History of WVU Women's Basketball," *WVUSports.com*, www.wvusports.com/content/files/Gamenotes/wbasketball/wvu history2014.

68 Back in 1973, athletic . . . tied at the waist.: "The History of WVU Women's Basketball."

68 [Girls high school basketball] had just . . . know much about the game.: "The History of WVU Women's Basketball."

69 Jay Rockefeller asked him . . . to build a first-class facility.: Nehlen with Poe, *Tales from the West Virginia Mountaineer Sideline*, pp. 12-13.

69 So Rockefeller invited him . . . passed the cards around again.: Nehlen with Poe, *Tales from the West Virginia Mountaineer Sideline*, p. 13.

69 This time, Thomas took his . . . $80,000 extra, didn't I?": Nehlen with Poe, *Tales from the West Virginia Mountaineer Sideline*, pp. 13-14.

69 Gosh dang it, if this guy would have turned his card in, we'd have had enough.": Nehlen with Poe, *Tales from the West Virginia Mountaineer Sideline*, p. 13.

70 the nation's lowest ranked undefeated team at No. 9.: Austin Murphy, "Mountain Pique," *Sports Illustrated*, Nov. 29, 1993, p. 20.

70 and ranked No. 4. . . . hunt for the national title.: Murphy, "Mountain Pique," p. 20.

70 a hole opened up by . . . took out two linebackers," Murphy, "Mountain Pique," p. 21.

70 the Mountaineers jumped to . . . the *USA/Today/CNN* poll.: Murphy, "Mountain Pique," p. 20.

70 For nine weeks, we got no respect.: Murphy, "Mountain Pique," p. 20.

71 He started out by . . . and caught on like crazy.: Jake Stump, "The Legend of the Flying WV," *WVU Magazine*, www.wvumag.edu/features/older/the-legend-of-the-flying-wv.

71 I wanted a distinct helmet.: Stump, "The Legend of the Flying WV."

72 Deniz Kilicli sat out . . . professional player on it.: Antonik, *Roll Out the Carpet*, p. 247.

72 WVU's starting lineup that . . . York City metropolitan area.: Antonik, *Roll Out the Carpet*, p. 251.

72 the Mountaineers had one . . . lead by three points.: Antonik, *Roll Out the Carpet*, p. 253.

72 In the East Regional finals . . . The team was 0-for-16.: Antonik, *Roll Out the Carpet*, p. 255.

73 "I honestly don't think I'm . . . of the next opponent.: Ivan Maisel, "Geno Smith: Football Nerd," *ESPN.com*, Oct. 3, 2012, http://www.espn.com/college-football/story/_/page/football-121003Maisel/west-virginia-mountaineers-quarterback-geno-smith-focus-solely-football.

73 90 percent of the game . . . the right decision.: Maisel, "Geno Smith: Football Nerd."

74 He is credited by some . . . parts of the state.: "Former WVU Coach Jim Carlen Dies," *BlueGoldNews*, July 22, 2012, http://www.scout.com/college/west-virginia/story/1204448-former-wvu-coach-jim-carlen-dies.

74 WVU's offense was in . . . "They never even touched him,": Mike Casazza, "A Look Back at Jim Carlen," *Charleston Gazette Mail*, July 22, 2012, http://blogs.wvgazettemail/wvu/2012/07/22/a-look-back-at-jim-carlen.

74 South Carolina had never seen us do that.: Casazza, "A Look Back at Jim Carlen."

75 "The expectations from media, . . . something we can control,": Connor Hicks, "Seniors Leave Lasting Mark," *The Daily Athenaeum*, March 16, 2016, http://www.thedaonline.com/sports/article_60960b36.

75 he set about fulfilling the promise he had made to rebuild the WVU dynasty.: "Jon Hammond, Head Coach," *WVUSports.com*, http://www.wvusports.com/staffDirectory.cfm?func=view&staffID=2122.

75 I came [to WVU] because . . . to win a national title.: Hicks, "Seniors Leave Lasting Mark."

76 "the WVU Coliseum still stands . . . showrooms for college basketball.": "WVU Coliseum," *WVUSports.com*, www.wvusports.com/page.cfm?section=7925.

76 The idea for a new basketball . . . request was largely ignored.: Antonik, *Roll Out the Carpet*, p. 134.

76 By the mid-1960s, though . . . site the following week.: Antonik, *Roll Out the Carpet*, p. 135.

76 You can kiss the Mountaineer basketball tradition good-bye.: Antonik, *Roll Out the Carpet*, p. 132.

77 There were 11 minutes remaining . . . of time could save West Virginia.": Meyer, "No Standing Pat."

77 "a gangly freshman about . . . whispered but little was known": Meyer, "No Standing Pat."

77 A play that was supposed to . . . for an unsuspecting program.: Meyer, "No Standing Pat."

78 As an undergrad at Ohio . . . and they loved him for it.: Antonik, *The Backyard Brawl*, p. 29.

78 When Huff was a junior . . . in front of the team.": Antonik, *The Backyard Brawl*, pp. 29-30.

79 Head coach Dana Holgorsen kept . . . top of my face mask.": Justin Jackson, "It Goes Without Seeing," *The Dominion Post*, Oct. 1, 2016, http://www.thedpost.com/it-goes-without-seeing-gibson-c.

79 I was watching the replay . . . seen it 20 times.: Jackson, "It Goes Without Seeing."

80 Some wags claimed that WVU . . . easiest job in the country: Antonik, *Roll Out the Carpet*, p. 118.

80   "just waited to see . . . another basketball All-American.": Antonik, *Roll Out the Carpet*, p. 118.

80   who once dove into the Ohio River to save a drowning woman: Antonik, *Roll Out the Carpet*, p. 108.

80   Despite some dogged persistence . . . to do a feature on West.: Antonik, *Roll Out the Carpet*, p. 93.

80   Jerry [West] was kept under wraps. He [was] taken out of games early.: Lazenby, *Jerry West*, p. 136.

81   had played quarterback . . . on the baseball team.: "Death of WVU Football Player: The Varsity Captain Killed," *Morgantown New Dominion*, Nov. 14, 1910, reprinted in *West Virginia Division of Culture and History: West Virginia Archives and History*, http://www.wvculture.org/history/sports/wvufootball03.html.

81   With WVU threatening to . . . conjecture to this day.: Ken Durbin, "The Captain That Gave His Life for WVU Football," *HailWV.com*, Aug. 22, 2012, http://hailwv.com/2012/08/22/the-captain-that-gave-his-life-for-wvu-football/.

81   Bethany's right end, whose name . . . down at the injured player.: "Death of WVU Football Player: The Varsity Captain Killed."

81   Testimony was inconclusive as to . . . and get him out of the game.: Durbin, "The Captain."

81   Subsequent investigations revealed . . . three weeks earlier.: "Death of WVU Football Player: The Varsity Captain Killed."

81   died without regaining consciousness . . . base of the cerebellum.: Durbin, "The Captain."

81   Indignation and anger ran . . . charging McCoy with murder.: "Death of WVU Football Player: The Varsity Captain Killed."

81   Two days after the . . . remainder of the season.: "Death of WVU Football Player: Accidental Death Verdict," *Morgantown New Dominion*, Nov. 15, 1910, reprinted in *West Virginia Division of Culture and History: West Virginia Archives and History*, http://www.wvculture.org/history/sports/wvufootball04.html.

81   There is a great demand . . . result of the game?: "Death of WVU Football Player: Who is Guilty?" *Morgantown New Dominion*, Nov. 18, 1910, reprinted in *West Virginia Division of Culture and History: West Virginia Archives and History*, http://www.wvculture.org/history/sports/wvufootball05.html.

82   The Las Vegas oddsmakers declared Florida to be the lock of the bowl season.: Antonik, *West Virginia University Football Vault*, p. 104.

82   "I thought we had a . . . got better all the time.": Nehlen with Poe, *Tales from the West Virginia Mountaineers Sideline*, p. 77.

82   Nehlen and his captains, . . . knew about the insult.: Nehlen with Poe, *Tales from the West Virginia Mountaineers Sideline*, p. 77.

82   The defensive coaches came up . . . plays and stuck with it.: Antonik, *West Virginia University Football Vault*, p. 104.

82   They also drew up a screen pass to running back Mickey Walczak: Nehlen with Poe, *Tales from the West Virginia Mountaineers Sideline*, p. 77.

82   Coach, I'm telling you [he] will know your name after the game is over.: Nehlen with Poe, *Tales from the West Virginia Mountaineers Sideline*, p. 77.

83   Garcia called being the mascot "the coolest thing I'll ever do in my life.": David Statman, "A Day in the Life of the West Virginia Mountaineer," *CAMPUSRUSH.com*, Oct. 7, 2015, http://www.campusrush.com/west-virginia-mountaineers-mascot-1392807639.html.

83   mascot Jonathan Kimble traveled . . . Virginia on his back.": Laura Wilcox Rote, "The Year of the Mountaineer," *Morgantown*, Aug.-Sept. 2012, http://www.morgantownmag.com/morgantown/August-September-2012/The-Year-of-the-Mountaineer/.

83   Our Mountaineer embodies . . . than other school mascots.: Rote, "The Year of the Mountaineer."

84   Izzo-Brown's first question when . . . the respect they deserved.: Katie Griffith, "Started from the Bottom, Now She's Here," *Morgantown*, Aug.-Sept. 2015, http://www.morgantownmag.com/morgantown/August-September-2015/Started-From-the-Bottom-Now-Shes-Here/.

84   "We do not choose . . . which we will stand.": R. Alan Culpepper, "The Gospel of Luke: Introduction, Commentary, and Reflections," *The New Interpreter's Bible*, Vol. IX (Nashville: Abingdon Press, 1998), p. 153.

85   Devine's maternal grandmother introduced . . . being a boy long ago: Dan DeLuca, "Noel Devine: The Long Run," *News-press.com*, Sept. 4, 2015, http://www.news-press.com/story/sports/2015/09/04/noel-devine-long-run/71699708/.

85   Life is too short to . . . forgive and forget.: DeLuca, "Noel Devine: The Long Run."

86   the Liberty Bowl's first . . . center, bowl officials jumped.: Antonik, *The Backyard Brawl*, p. 91.

86   a four-inch thick grass . . . could watch the grass grow.: Antonik, *The Backyard Brawl*, pp. 91-92.

86   The end zones were eight . . . the game . . . Thank God!": Antonik, *The Backyard Brawl*, p. 92.

86   WVU chose to defend the . . . Miss America pageant stage.: Antonik, *The Backyard Brawl*, p. 92.

87   "I just got that . . . outwork [the scholarshipped players],": Antonik, *The Backyard Brawl*, p. 213.

200

87 One day as Nehlen left . . . I give it away,": Antonik, *The Backyard Brawl*, p. 213.

87 I had to walk about . . . with all those vegetables.: Antonik, *The Backyard Brawl*, p. 213.

88 Misfortune struck early when . . . was felled by the flu.: Antonik, *Roll out the Carpet*, p. 11.

88 He was eventually transferred back to Morgantown.: Antonik, *Roll out the Carpet*, p. 11.

88 the flu sent guard Russ Meredith [. . .] back home.: Antonik, *Roll out the Carpet*, p. 11.

88 forward Pierre Hill and center Roy "Legs Hawley" [. . .] were stricken.: Antonik, *Roll out the Carpet*, p. 11.

88 Down to only five players . . . any more healthy players.: Antonik, *Roll out the Carpet*, p. 11.

88 It was a trip filled with misadventure.: Antonik, *Roll out the Carpet*, p. 11.

89 The WVU Marching Band was first . . . marching band for that year.: "WVU Marching Band History," *theprideofwestvirginia*.org, http://theprideofwestvirginia.org/about_the_band/marching-band-history.html.

90 McAfee decided to concentrate . . . offered him a scholarship.: Zak Keefer, "$100, a Lie and a Poker Club," *Indianapolis Star*, Oct. 24, 2014, http://www.indystar.com/story/sports/nfl/colts/2014/10/24/how-pat-mcafee-became-an-nfl-punter.

90 If I'd ended up at . . . if I'd even have kicked?: Keefer, "$100, a Lie and a Poker Club."

91 he changed the team's . . . Bluefield boys to Virginia Tech,": Antonik, *West Virginia University Football Vault*, p. 86.

91 [Jim Carlen] liked to have his fingers in everything.: Antonik, *West Virginia University Football Vault*, p. 86.

92 Each day after practice, . . . leverage from her height: "Georgeann Wells," *Wikipedia, the free encyclopedia*, http://en.wikipedia.orga/wiki/Georgeann-Wells.

92 With WVU comfortably ahead, . . . Naismith Basketball Hall of Fame.: "The History of WVU Women's Basketball."

92 Unmatched until 1994, . . . most talked about accomplishments.: "The History of WVU Women's Basketball."

93 He required his WVU teams . . . took a lot of clothes.": Antonik, *West Virginia University Football Vault*, p. 34.

93 Just how sensitive he was. . . another fundraising event in Huntington.: Antonik, *West Virginia University Football Vault*, pp. 34, 37.

93 After the 1924 season, . . . his medical career,: Antonik, *West Virginia University Football Vault*, p. 33.

93 The possibilities for my down, as I left.: Antonik, *West Virginia University Football Vault*, p. 33.

94 "We shoot to get . . . got three by himself.": Joey Lomonaco, "WVU's Joseph a Ball-Hawking Bandit," *TheDPost.com*, Sept. 6, 2015, http://thedpost.com/9-7-JOSEPH.

94 His reaction to the . . . at how silly the stat sounded.: Lomonaco, "WVU's Joseph."

94 That's amazing, and that's all I can say.: Lomonaco, "WVU's Joseph."

95 One Sunday night in October . . . as he once had.: Nehlen with Poe, *Tales from the West Virginia Mountaineers Sideline*, p. 163.

95 When he got home, he told . . . and told him the news.: Nehlen with Poe, *Tales from the West Virginia Mountaineers Sideline*, p. 164.

95 he announced that none of coaches on Nehlen's staff would be retained.: Antonik, *West Virginia University Football Vault*, p. 118.

95 Nehlen wasn't sure the coaches . . . really didn't want to do it.: Nehlen with Poe, *Tales from the West Virginia Mountaineers Sideline*, p. 167.

95 Nehlen said the practices leading up to the bowl game were "miserable.": Antonik, *West Virginia University Football Vault*, p. 118.

95 We had lousy practices . . . "Things didn't look good.": Nehlen with Poe, *Tales from the West Virginia Mountaineers Sideline*, p. 167.

95 It's time to let somebody . . . watch games on television.: Antonik, *West Virginia University Football Vault*, p. 118.

WORKS USED

Adelson, Andrea. "West Virginia Back in Thick of Big East Race." *ESPN.com*. 13 Nov. 2011. http://www.espn.com/blog/bigeast/post/_/id/26398/west-virginia-back-in-thick-of-big-east-race.

Anderson, Holly. "Geno Smith, West Virginia Outlast Baylor in Historic Big 12 Shootout." *SI.com*. 30 Sept. 2012. http://www.si.com/college-football/campus-union/2012/09/29/west-virginia-baylor-geno-smith-big-12.

Antonik, John. "30 Most Unforgettable Games." *WVUsports.com*. 25 July 2010. http://www.wvusports.com/30Games.cfm?story=16786.

-----. "2006 Sugar Bowl: Dan Mozes." *WVUsports.com*. http://www.wvusports.com/blogs.cfm?blog=footballBlog&story=28140.

-----. "2006 Sugar Bowl: Owen Schmitt." *WVUsports.com*. http://www.wvusports.com/page.cfm?story=28160.

-----. *Roll out the Carpet: 101 Seasons of West Virginia University Basketball*. Morgantown: West Virginia University Press, 2010.

-----. *The Backyard Brawl: Stories from One of the Weirdest, Wildest, Longest Running, and Most Intensive Rivalries in College Football History*. Morgantown: West Virginia University Press, 2012.

-----. *West Virginia University Football Vault: The History of the Mountaineers*. Atlanta: Whitman Publishing LLC, 2009.

-----. "WVU Football: A Band of Brothers." *WVUsports.com*. 30 June 2016. http://www.wvusports.com/page.cfm?story=30379&cat=football.

-----. "WVU Men's Soccer Turns 50." *MSNSports.NET.com*. 30 Aug. 2010. http://wvutoday.wvu.edu/n/2010/8/30/wvu-men-s-soccer-turns-50.

-----. "WVU Sports Hall of Fame: Jerry West." *WVUsports.com*. http://www.wvusports.com/hallOfFame.cfm?func=viewProfile&hofID=49.

Burns, Marty. "Amos Zereoue West Virginia's Fast-Forward Sophomore Tailback." *Sports Illustrated*. 6 Oct. 1997. http://www.si.com/vault/1997/10/06/232764/amos-zereoue-west-virginias-fast-forward-sophomore-tailback.

Casazza, Mike. "A Look Back at Jim Carlen." *Charleston Gazette-Mail*. 22 July 2012. http://blogs.wvgazettemail.com/wvu/2012/07/22/a-look-back-at-jim-carlen.

-----. "Man of the (Early) Hour: Mike Carey." *Charleston Gazette-Mail*. 3 March 2014. http://blogs.www.gazettemail.com/wvu/2014/03/03/man-of-the-hour-mike-carey.

-----. *Waiting for the Fall: A Decade of Dreams, Drama and West Virginia University Football*. St. Paul, Minn.: Stance & Speed LLC: 2012.

-----. "WVU Football Opens with Win Against Missouri." *Charleston Gazette-Mail*. 3 Sept. 2016. http://www.wvgazettemail.com/sports/wvu/20160903/wvu-football-opens-with-win-against-missouri.

Constantine, Tony with Dan Miller. *Mountaineer Football 1891-1969*. Morgantown: Athletic Publicity Office West Virginia University, 1969.

"Country Roads: Take Me Home, Country Roads." *WVUsports.com*. http://www.wvusports.com/page.cfm?section=23881.

Culpepper, R. Alan. "The Gospel of Luke: Introduction, Commentary, and Reflections." *The New Interpreter's Bible*. Vol. IX. Nashville: Abingdon Press, 1998. 1-490.

Curtis, Tara. "Hall of Famer and WVU Great Major Harris to lead Homecoming Parade." *WVUtoday.edu*. 14 Oct. 2010. http://wvutoday.edu/n/2010/10/14/hall-of-famer-and-wvu-great-major-harris-to-lead-homecoming-parade.

"Death of WVU Football Player: Accidental Death Verdict in the Case of Captain Munk." *Morgantown New Dominion*. 15 Nov. 1910. Reprinted in *West Virginia Division of Culture and History: West Virginia Archives and History*, http://www.wvculture.org/history/sports/wvufootball04.html.

"Death of WVU Football Player: The Varsity Captain Killed." *Morgantown New Dominion*. 14 Nov. 1910. Reprinted in *West Virginia Division of Culture and History: West*

Virginia Archives and History, http://www.wvculture.org/history/sports/wvu football03.html.

"Death of WVU Football Player: Who Is Guilty in the Death of Captain Munk?" *Morgantown New Dominion*. 18 Nov. 1910. Reprinted in *West Virginia Division of Culture and History: West Virginia Archives and History*, http://www.wvculture.org/history/sports/wvufootball05.html.

DeLuca, Dan. "Noel Devine: The Long Run." *News-press.com*. 4 Sept. 2015. http://www.news-press.com/story/sports/2015/09/04/noel-devine-long-run/71699708/.

Dinich, Heather. "Clemson Collapses on ACC's Biggest Stage." *ESPN.com*. 5 Jan. 2012. http://www.espn.com/blog/acc/post/_/id/35295/clemson-collapses-on-accs-biggest-stage.

"Double Life: Standout WVU Linebacker Reed Williams Excels in Academics Too." *wvu today*. 23 Sept. 2009. http://wvutoday.com/wvu.edu/n/2009/12/23/double-life-standout-wvu-linebacker-excells-in-academics-too.

Durbin, Ken. "16 — Todd Sauerbrun." *West Virginia 100 Day Countdown to Victory*. 16 Aug. 2012. http://wvu100countdown.blogspot.com/2012/08/16-todd-sauerbrun.html.

-----. "The Captain That Gave His Life for WVU Football." *HailWV.com*. 22 Aug. 2012. http://hailwv.com/2012/08/22/the-captain-that-gave-his-life-for-wvu-football/.

Evans, Thayer. "Holgorsen's Long But Tumultuous Journey." *FOXSports*. 23 Sept. 2011. http://msn.foxsports.com/collegefootball/story/west-virginia-mountaineers-coach-dana-holgorsen.

"Fights Songs and Chants: First Down Cheer." *WVUsports.com*. http://www.wvusports.com/page.cfm?section=13065.

Finder, Chuck. "Chunky Child Has Grown into Leader of West Virginia's Stingy Defense." *Pittsburgh Post-Gazette*. 14 Oct. 2007. http://www.post-gazette.com/sports/wvu/2007/10/14/Chunky-child-has-grown-into-leader-of-West-Virginia-s-stingy-defense/stories/200710140175.

-----. "Gator Bowl: West Virginia Rallies to Beat Georgia Tech." *Pittsburgh Post-Gazette*. 2 Jan. 2007. http://www.post-gazette.com/sports/wvu/2007/01/02/Gator-Bowl-West-Virginia-rallies-to-beat-Georgia Tech/stories/200701020170.

"Former WVU Coach Jim Carlen Dies." *BlueGoldNews*. 22 July 2012. http://www.scout.com/college/west-virginia/story/1204448-former-wvu-coach-jim-carlen-dies.

Frank, Martin. "Delaware Native Wendell Smallwood: 'Football Saved My Life.'" *The News Journal*. 22 July 2016. http://www.delawareonline.com/story/sports/nfl/eagles/2016/07/22/delaware-native-wendell-smallwood-football-saved-my-life/87443314/.

"Fred Wyant." *Wikipedia, the free encyclopedia*. https://en.wikipedia.org/wiki/Fred_Wyant.

Furfari, Mickey. "Dunlevy Was an Outstanding Receiver at WVU." *The Times West Virginian*. 22 July 2015. http://www.timeswv.com/sports/furfari-column-dunlevy-was-an-outstanding-receiver-at-wvu/article_0b95d658.

-----. "Kinder First of Only Two Ever to Wear 100 on Jersey." *Bluefield Daily Telegraph*. 24 Sept. 2013. http://www.bdtonline.com/sports/sports_columns/kinder-first-of-only-two-ever-to-wear-on-jersey/article.

-----. "Rodgers Was Mountaineers' Greatest All-Around Athlete." *The Register-Herald*. 19 March 2013. http://www.register-herald.com/collegesports/x765714564.

-----. "WVU Kicker Wore No. 100 Proudly." *The Register-Herald*. 27 March 2013. http://www.register-herald.com/todayssportsfront/x1485886127/WVU-kicker-wore-No-100-proudly.

"Geno Smith Throws for 656 Yards, 8 TDs in WVU's Wild 70-63 Win." *ESPN.go.com*. 29 Sept. 2012. http://scores.espn.go.com/ncf/recap?gameId=32273077.

"Georgeann Wells." *Wikipedia, the free encyclopedia*. http://en.wikipedia.org/wiki/Georgeann_Wells.

Glicksman, Ben. "The Evolution of West Virginia WR and NFL Draft Prospect Kevin White." *Sports Illustrated*. 19 Nov. 2014. http://www.

si.com/college-football/2014/11/19/kevin-white-west-virginia-mountaineers.

Griffith, Katie. "Started from the Bottom, Now She's Here." *Morgantown.* Aug.-Sept. 2015. http://www.morgantownmag.com/morgantown/August-September-2015/Started-From-the-Bottom-Now-Shes-Here/.

Hays, Graham. "Amanda Hill Leans on Brother's Love." *ESPN.com.* 31 Oct. 2012. http://www.espn.com/espnw/news-commentary/article/8568799/espnw-west-virginia-mountaineers-midfielder-amanda-hill-leans-brother-love.

Herter, Eric. "What a Great Setting for Some Football." *Believe: The Story of the 2007 West Virginia Mountaineer Football Team.* Morgantown: *The Dominion Post,* 2008. 10-11.

Hertzel, Bob. "Howard Shows His Toughness in Opener." *The Exponent Telegram.* 3 Sept. 2016. http://www.theet.com/sports/wvu/howard-shows-his-toughness-in-opener/article.

Hicks, Connor. "Seniors Leave Lasting Mark on Renowned Mountaineers Program." *The Daily Athenaeum.* 16 March 2016, http://www.thedaonline.com/sports/article_60960b36.

"The History of WVU Women's Basketball." *WVUSports.com.* www.wvusports.com/content/files/Gamenotes/wbasketball/wvuhistory2014.

"Hot Rod Hundley." *Wikipedia, the free encyclopedia.* https://en.wikipedia.org/wiki/Hot_Rod_Hundley.

Jackson, Justin. "It Goes Without Seeing: Gibson Catch Was Huge." *The Dominion Post.* 1 Oct. 2016. http://www.thedpost.com/it-goes-without-seeing-gibson-c.

"Joe Alexander." *Wikipedia, the free encyclopedia.* https://en.wikipedia.org/wiki/Joe_Alexander.

"Jon Hammond, Head Coach." *WVUSports.com.* http://www.wvusports.com/staffDirectory.cfm?func=view&staffID=2122.

Keefer, Zac. "$100, a Lie and a Poker Club: How Pat McAfee Became an NFL Punter." *Indianapolis Star.* 24 Oct. 2014. http://www.indystar.com/story/sports/nfl/colts/2014/10/24/how-pat-mcafee-became-an-nfl-punter.

Lazenby, Roland. *Jerry West: The Life and Legend of a Basketball Icon.* New York: Ballentine Books, 2009.

Loh, Stefanie. "Un-bowl-ievable." *Believe: The Story of the 2007 West Virginia Mountaineer Football Team.* Morgantown: *The Dominion Post,* 2008. 139.

-----. "Williams Creates a Scene." *Believe: The Story of the 2007 West Virginia Mountaineer Football Team.* Morgantown: *The Dominion Post,* 2008. 71-72.

Lomonaco, Joey. "WVU Trounces Terrapins, 45-6." *TheDPost.com.* 26 Sept. 2015. http://thedpost.com/WVU-trounces-Terrap--ins,-45-6.

-----. "WVU's Joseph a Ball-Hawking Bandit." *TheDPost.com.* 6 Sept. 2015. http://thedpost.com/9-7-JOSEPH.

Maese, Rick. "Ginny Thrasher Picked Up a Gun Four Years Ago; Now She Has a Shooting Gold Medal." *The Washington Post.* 6 Aug. 2016, http://www.washingtonpost.com/sports/olympics/ginny-thrasher-picked-up-a-gun-four-years-ago.

Maisel, Ivan. "Geno Smith: Football Nerd." *ESPN.com.* 3 Oct. 2012. http://www.espn.com/college-football/story/_/page/football-121003Maisel/west-virginia-mountaineers-quarterback/geno-smith-focus-solely-football.

Mascaro, Chris. "Brawl Breaks Out at Hawaii-West Virginia Women's Basketball Game." *SI.com.* 18 Nov. 2013. http://www.si.com/si-wire/2013/11/18/brawl-breaks-out-at-hawaii-west-virginia-womens-basketball-game.

Meyer, Craig. "No Standing Pat." *Pittsburgh Post-Gazette.* http://newsineractive.post-gazette.com/oral-history/west-virginia/.

"Mountaineer Mantrip." *WVUsports.com.* http://www.wvusports.com/page.cfm?section=21564.

Murphy, Austin. "Mountain Pique." *Sports Illustrated.* 29 Nov. 1993. 20-21.

Murray, Todd. "Mountaineers Hold Off BYU in Thriller." *The Dominion Post.* 24 Sept. 2016. http://www.thedpost.com/mountaineers/hold-off-byu-in-thriller.

-----. "WVU RB Smallwood Exacts Revenge on Terps." *TheDPost.com.* 26 Sept. 2015. http://

thedpost.com/Smallwood-exacts-revenge-on-Te.

Nehlen, Don with Shelly Poe. *Tales from the West Virginia Mountaineers Sideline: A Collection of the Greatest Mountaineers Stories Ever Told.* Sports Publishing: New York City, 2012.

"Owen Schmitt." *Wikipedia, the free encyclopedia.* http://en.wikipedia.org/wiki/Owen_Schmitt.

"Roll Out the Carpet: Let's Roll Out the Carpet." *WVUsports.com.* http://www.wvusports.com/page.cfm?section=23880.

Rote, Laura Wilcox. "The Year of the Mountaineer." *Morgantown.* August-September 2012. http://www.morgantownmag.com/morgantown/August-September-2012/The-Year-of-the-Mountaineer/.

Rubenstein, Drew. "Stewart Deserves a Serious Look." *Believe: The Story of the 2007 West Virginia Mountaineer Football Team.* Morgantown: *The Dominion Post,* 2008. 157.

Southern, Patrick. "A Storied History: 1988 WVU Football Team." *The DAonline.com.* 3 Oct. 2008. http://www.thedaonline.com/article_461a3063.

Staples, Andy. "Centered by Fatherhood, Will Grier Is Enjoying the Final Year of His Winding College Career." *SI.com.* 30 Oct. 2018. https://www.si.com/college-football/2018/10/30/will-grier-family-daughter-west-virginia-mountaineers.

Statman, David. "A Day in the Life of the West Virginia Mountaineer: The Mascot Who Can't Hide His Face." *CAMPUSRUSH.com.* 7 Oct. 2015. http://www.campusrush.com/west-virginia-mountaineers-mascote-1392807639.html.

Stump, Jake. "The Legend of the Flying WV." *WVU Magazine.* www.wvumag.edu/features/older/the-legend-of-the-flying-wv.

"Tarik Phillip's Clutch 3 Seals Win for West Virginia over Buffalo." *ESPN.com.* 21 March 2015. http://cdn.espn.com/ncb/recap?da,eId=400785436.

Toquinto, Jeff. "From the Bench: 25 Years Later, Major Harris Talks Value of 'The Play' and Resuming the PSU Series." *connectBridgeport.com.* 4 Aug. 2013, http://www.connect-bridgeport.com/connect.cfm?func=view&section=Sports-Blog&item=From-the-Bench-25-Years-Later-Major-Harris-Talks-Value.

Trinone, Angelica. "Father and Son Share Success on the Court." *WValways.* 29 Jan. 2016. http://www.wvalways.com/story/31095993/father-and-son-share-success.

Trotter, Jake. "From Seventh-Grade Phenom to Failed QB to Elite Receiver." *ESPN.com.* 6 Oct. 2017. http://www.espn.com/college-football/story/_/id/20923614.west-virginia-david-sills-7th-grade-phenom-failed-qb-elite-receiver.

-----. "Rasul Douglas' Journey to Becoming the Big 12's Best DB." *ESPN.com.* 17 Nov. 2016. http://www.espn.com/college-football/story/_/id/18070582/west-virginia-mountaineers-rasul-doouglas-hourney-become-big-12-best-db.

"West Virginia Routs Clemson in Record-Setting Orange Bowl." *ESPN.com.* 4 Jan. 2012. http://cdn.espn.com/ncf/recap?gameId=320040228.

Wetzel, Dan. "W.Va. Coach Huggins Keeps Bouncing Back." *YAHOO!Sports.* 26 May 2010. http://rivals.yahoo.com/ncaa/basketball/news.

Whiteford, Mike. "The Road Not Traveled." *The Charleston Gazette.* 24 June 2010. http://www.wvgazette.com/Sports/WVU/201006241018.

Wiley, Ralph. "Major Harris Rose From Pittsburgh's Hill District to Football Heights." *SI.com.* 19 Dec. 1988. http://www.si.com/vault/1988/12/19/119089/showdown-in-the-fiesta-bowl.

"WVU Coliseum." *WVUSports.com.* www.wvusports.com/page.cfm?section=7925.

"WVU Escapes Sooners after Buddy Hield's Half-Court Heave Waved Off." *ESPN.com.* 12 March 2016. http://cdn.espn.com/ncb/recap?gameId=400870832.

"WVU Marching Band History." *theprideofwestvirginia.org.* http://theprideofwestvirginia.org/about_the_band/marching-band-history.html.

WEST VIRGINIA

NAME INDEX
(LAST NAME, DEVOTION DAY NUMBER)

Abraham, Zach 30, 87
Adams, Jacquez 8
Adams, Jordan 8
Akers, Willie 33
Alexander, Joe 56
Alston, Shawne 59
Antonik, John 2, 13, 14, 30, 51, 57, 61, 88
Arnold, Boyd H. 83
Austin, Tavon 22, 59
Babic, Melica 75
Bailey, Stedman 50, 59
Baker, Mike 70
Barrett, Eddie 80, 91
Barrows, Scott 43
Bauer, Dan 44
Beach Boys 5
Beck, Curlin 62
Bednarik, Adam 14, 31, 77
Bennett, Rob 43
Bitancurt, Tyler 22
Bivens, Robert F. 1
Blake, Devon 63
Blakemore, Kittie 68
Bosley, Bruce 80
Bowden, Bobby 15, 26, 67
Boyd, Betty 91
Boyd, Tajh 42
Brady, Phil 45
Braham, Rich 70
Branch, Andre 42
Braxton, Jim 74
Brown, Red 76
Bryant, Truck 72
Buie, Andrew 50
Bussie, Asya 7
Butler, Da'Sean 72
Byrd, Leland 18, 61
Caldwell, Christal 7
Campbell, Jonah 8
Campbell, Shea 8
Carey, Cheryl 7
Carey, Mike 7
Carlen, Jim 26, 41, 74, 91
Carter, Jevon 48
Casazza, Mike 19, 37, 45, 65
Castillo, Randy 89
Catlett, Gale 11, 28
Chugunov, Chris 8
Chugunov, Mitch 8
Cignetti, Frank 18
Clarkson, Steve 27

Clemons, Troy 83
Coale, Sherri 5
Cobourne, Avon 85
Colvard, Fred 49
Constantine, Tony 54
Cook, Darwin 42
Corum, Gene 6, 26, 32, 49
Cousin Itt 21
Crane, Russ 49
Crest, William 94
Culpepper, R. Alan 84
Curtis, Tara 46
Dakich, Dan 28
Dangerfield, Rodney 70
Davis, J.B. 88
Dawson, Mike 18
DeGroot, Dudley 21, 57
DeJarnett, Dave 43
Denver, John 25
Devine, Noel 2, 85
Dillon, KJ 94
Dinich, Heather 42
Dixon, Ed 84
Dooley, Vince 34
Douglas, Rasul 47
Duda, Mark 63
Dunlap, Steve 29
Dunlevy, Bob 6, 86
Durante, Jovon 79, 94
Durst, Rebecca 83
Ellis, Theron 29
Emory, Frederick L. 1
Ebanks, Devin 72
Feller, Bob 1
Ferns, Brendan 8
Ferns, Michael 8
Fields, Averee 37
Fleming, Jack 3, 25, 32
Fleming, Maurice 17
Flick, Jim 74
Garcia, Michael 83
Garrison, Dustin 50
Gibson, Shelton 79
Gibson, Tony 47, 90
Gonzalez, Tito 2, 53
Goode, Najee 22
Gratz, Elizabeth 75
Gresham, Bob 74
Grier, Rosey 78
Grier, Will 36
Hamilton, Scott 3
Hammond, Jon 75
Hampton, Brooke 7

Harlow, James 44
Harrick, Steve 26
Harris, Major 13, 46
Hawkins, Robert 88
Hawley, Roy 21, 54, 88
Herock, Ken 49
Herter, Eric 58
Hicks, Roger 3
Hield, Buddy 48
Hill, Amanda 60
Hill, Bobby 34
Hill, Dan 60
Hill, Lori 60
Hill, Pierre 88
Hoffman, Richard 32
Holdinsky, Roger 49
Holgorsen, Dana 4, 8, 12, 17, 27, 38, 47, 50, 59, 73, 79
Holgorsen, Logan 8
Holgorsen, Steve 8
Holmes, John 53
Holton, Jonathan 48
Hostetler, Jeff 43, 62
Howard, Skyler 4, 17, 38, 79, 94
Huff, Sam 78, 80
Huggins, Bob 24, 56, 64
Hundley, Hot Rod 16, 44, 52, 72, 80
Izzo-Brown, Nikki 60, 84
Jay, Ben 7
Johnston, Chad 30, 66
Jones, Greg 11
Jones, Kevin 72
Jordan, Michael 56
Joseph, Karl 94
Jozwiak, Brian 43
Juskowich, Ken 41
Kehl, Kurt 43
Kendra, Dan 15
Kerin, Mike 71
Kern, Bill 21, 32
Kesling, Dick 3
Kiess, Trevor 83
Kiffin, Lane 27
Kilicli, Deniz 72
Kimble, Jon 50, 83
Kinder, Carl 26, 41
Kosanovich, Eli 49
Lamone, Gene 57
Lawrence, Jennifer 21
Lazenby, Roland 16
Leach, Mike 12

Leary, Crystal 37
Legg, Bill 43
Lewis, Art 9, 21, 39, 57, 78
Lewis, C.S. 23
Lewis, Johnny 9
Lewis, Mary Belle 9
Lockwood, Dave 29, 46
Lombardi, Vince 14, 29
Lomonaco, Joey 4
Lucas, Jean-Pierre 75
Luck, Oliver 10, 12, 18, 82
Mahrt, Armin 5
Maisel, Ivan 13
Mallory, John 91
Markel, Jim 40
Martin, Dick 55, 71
Martin, Homer 88
Martin, John 71
Mazzulla, Joe 56
McAfee, Pat 31, 53, 77, 90
McCoy 81
McElwain, Jim 36
McKenzie, Bill 15
Meredith, Russ 5, 67, 88
Mestrezat, Walter 89
Metzger, Sol 61
Meyer, Billy 1
Meyer, Craig 77
Miller, Darrell 62
Miller, Julian 22
Molina, Mike 79
Moore, Arch 91
Moran, Sonny 44
Mozes, Dan 14, 53
Mumme, Hal 12
Munk, Rudolph 81
Myers, Greg 41
Myles, Brandon 53
Nardacci, Nick 5, 49, 67
Nehlen, Don 10, 13, 25, 46, 55,
  62, 66, 69 71, 82, 84, 87, 95
Nehlen, Merry Ann 95
Noel, Patricia West 33
Nolan, Diane 68
Obie 42
Oblak, Dave 18
O'Neil, Jeanne 36
Ours, Wes 5
Paige, Jaysean 48
Parsons, Mike 71
Pastilong, Ed 95
Patrick, Oscar 74
Patrone, Lee 80
Phillip, Tarik 64
Phillips, Morgan 75
Post, Melville D. 1

Procopio, Jim 49
Pugh, Charles 53
Pushkin, Martin 40
Raese, Dyke 3
Randolph, Pat 43
Raugh, Mark 82
Ray, Rachael 87
Raynaud, Darius 45
Retton, Mary Lou 72
Reynolds, Ryan 21
Ribble, Lisa 92
Rice, Grantland 61
Richards, Bob 28
Richt, Mark 45
Rigg, Doug 22
Ringer, Lewis 40
Roberts, Sara 68
Robinson, Wil 28, 44
Rockefeller, Jay 25, 69
Rodgers, Ira 61, 67
Rodriguez, Rich 2, 14, 45,
  65, 95
Rogers, W. W. 81
Rogers, Williams 83
Rollins, Walter 3
Rossi, Ralph 40
Rote, Laura Wilcox 83
Ruth, Babe 9
Sarkisian, Steve 27
Sauerbrun, Todd 66
Sax, Steve 78
Schaus, Fred 33, 58
Schembechler, Bo 10, 55
Schmitt, Owen 2, 53, 65
Seider, Ja'HSaun 8
Seider, JaJuan 8
Sergy, Leslie 68
Setron, Joe 67
Shakespeare, William 1
Sharrar, Lloyd 80
Shell, Rushel 17, 38, 94
Shockey, Ed 9
Shorts, Jr., Daikiel 17
Sills, David V 27
Simons, Jack 5
Slaton, Steve 2, 45, 53, 65,
  77
Smallwood, Wendell 4, 23, 94
Smith, Chuck 15
Smith, Eain 59
Smith, Geno 22, 50, 59, 73
Smith, Red 86
Smith, Wellington 72
Sottile, Jim 16
Spears, Clarence 67, 93
Spurgeon, Garrett 75

Stadsvold, Francis 88
Stansbury, Harry 51, 93
Staten Juwan 64
Statler Brothers 13
Stepney, Linda 37
Stewart, Bill 2, 12
Stewart, Irvin 32
Stone, Jack 39
Stydahar, Joe 78
Sutton, Eddie 24
Swinson, Randy 15
Symons, Dick 44
Talley, Darryl 18
Tarkanian, Jerry 11
Tennant, Natalie 83
Thomas, Dwayne 23
Thomas, Orville 69
Thomas-Williams, Donte 94
Thorn, Joe 52
Thorn, Rod 52, 80
Thrasher, Ginny 20, 75
Trickett, Rick 14
Vance, Paul 61
Walczak, Mickey 82
Walker, Barbara 68
Walker, Robert 70
Washington, Vann 94
Waters, Bucky 76
Wells, Georgeann 92
West, Jarrod 28
West, Jerry 33, 44, 52, 72, 80
Wetzel, Dan 24
White, Ka'Raun 8
White, Kevin, Jr. 63
White, Kyzir 8
White, Pat 2, 14, 31, 53, 65,
  77, 85
White, Pete 54
Wicks, Eric 77
Williams, Devin 64
Williams, Eddie 74
Williams, Reed 34
Williams, Ron 56
Wolfley, Ron 43
Woodard, Rodney 70
Woods, Larry 28
Woodside, Paul 61
Workman, Mark 80
Wuerffel, Danny 84
Wyant, Fred 39
Yoke, Roy 93
Zereoue, Amos 35
Zereoue, Bonde 35

WEST VIRGINIA

SCRIPTURES INDEX
(by DEVOTION DAY NUMBER)

Acts 1:15-25	53	James 5:7-12	43
Acts 19:11-20	61		
		Jeremiah 1:4-10	7
1 Corinthians 9:24-27	22		
1 Corinthians 11:17-29	72	Job 1; 2:1-10	81
		Job 28	73
2 Corinthians 5:1-10	33		
2 Corinthians 5:6-10	79	John 1:43-51	21
2 Corinthians 5:11-21	34	John 2:12-23	45
2 Corinthians 7:8-13	13	John 4:27-42	11
2 Corinthians 11:21b-29	38	John 6:60-69	41
2 Corinthians 12:23-33	37	John 19:25-30	60
		John 20:11-18	36
Daniel 3	66		
		Joshua 3	20
Ephesians 4:17-24	40		
		1 Kings 10:1-10, 18-29	92
Exodus 22:1-15	94		
Exodus 26:31-35; 30:1-10	54	2 Kings 2:1-12	93
Exodus 32:1-20	17		
		Luke 5:1-11	68
Galatians 5:16-26	5	Luke 6:46-49	84
		Luke 13:31-35	62
Genesis 1; 2:1-3	1	Luke 15:1-10	15
Genesis 3:1-7, 21-24	14	Luke 20:9-19	82
Genesis 7	42	Luke 22:54-62	51
Genesis 9:1-7	87	Luke 23:26-43	24
Genesis 11:1-11	32		
Genesis 21:1-7	16	Mark 1:21-28	80
Genesis 37:1-11	78	Mark 3:1-12	50
		Mark 3:31-35	8
Hebrews 3:7-19	6	Mark 5:22-43	23
Hebrews 11:13-16	65	Mark 6:1-6	71
Hebrews 12:14-17	7	Mark 7:1-13	58
		Mark 8:31-38	70
Isaiah 53	25	Mark 9:33-37	46
		Mark 12:28-34	59
James 2:14-26	49	Mark 14:66-72	64

MOUNTAINEERS

Mark 15:16-32	83			
Mark 16:9-20	57	Philippians 1:3-14	85
		Philippians 2:1-11	28
Matthew 3:1-12	39	Philippians 3:10-16	52
Matthew 3:13-17	35			
Matthew 4:18-22	90	Psalm 42	77
Matthew 5:33-37	44	Psalm 98	89
Matthew 5:38-42	4	Psalm 102	18
Matthew 5:43-48	29			
Matthew 7:7-14	47	Revelation 21:22-27; 22:1-6	12
Matthew 8:18-22	19	Revelation 22:7-17	95
Matthew 9:35-38	56			
Matthew 12:38-42	2	Romans 2:1-16	74
Matthew 16:13-17	67	Romans 6:1-14	10
Matthew 16:21-23	63	Romans 8:28-30	30
Matthew 24:36-51	3	Romans 12:1-2	67
Matthew 25:1-13	48	Romans 12:9-21	86
Matthew 25:31-46	91	Romans 14:1-12	55
Matthew 26:14-16; 27:1-10	69			
		1 Samuel 28:3-20	9
Nahum 1:1-8	88			
		2 Samuel 7:1-7	76
Nehemiah 8:1-3, 9-12	26	2 Samuel 7:8-17	75
Numbers 13:25-14:4	31